The Colonial Image

Australian Painting 1800–1880

Eugene von Guérard
Ferntree Gully in the Dandenong Ranges 1857
   (detail)
oil on canvas
92.0 × 138.0 cm
Australian National Gallery

The Colonial Image

Australian Painting 1800–1880

Tim Bonyhady

Australian National Gallery
Ellsyd Press

Acknowledgements

In writing this book I have frequently relied on Roger Butler and Andrew Sayers who gave me great assistance in refining the idea for the book and helped select the paintings. Together with Claire Young, Anne Bonyhady and Helen Ennis, they also substantially improved the text, especially the introductory essay. After three-and-a-half years writing Australian art history in the relative isolation of Cambridge and Montreal, it is good to have the assistance and encouragement of friends and colleagues close at hand.

First published 1987 by Ellsyd Press, an imprint of David Ell Press Pty Ltd, 137–139 Regent Street, Chippendale 2008, Australia
Copyright © Tim Bonyhady
Design by Jane Parish
Typeset by Love Computer Typesetting, Sydney
Printed by The Craftsman Press, Melbourne
National Library of Australia
Cataloguing-in-Publication Data
Bonyhady, Tim, 1957–
   The colonial image: Australian painting 1800–1880.

   Bibliography.
   ISBN 0 949290 25 4.

   1. Painting, Australian 2. Painting, Modern — 19th century — Australia. I. Australian National Gallery. II. Title.

759.994

Preface

Over the past decade there has been a growing appreciation of the diversity of colonial painting. Public art galleries have increasingly acquired and displayed works other than landscapes and portraits of successful colonists. Exhibitions have been held of paintings of Aboriginals, 'house portraits', and sporting and animal pictures. Painters of still lifes, marine pictures and history subjects have, for the first time, been the subject of serious investigation.

The Australian National Gallery has played a significant role in this re-evaluation. Although still far from possessing a representative collection of colonial art, it has acquired major examples of colonial history painting, genre painting, group portraiture, large-scale ethnographic painting, still life and marine painting. Together with landscapes and more conventional portraits of the settlers, these works give some indication of the breadth of colonial painting.

This book, commissioned by the Gallery and based principally on its holdings, also draws on other collections in order to show the range of colonial painting. Although still emphasising landscape and portraiture, it shows that colonial artists painted a great diversity of subjects: from fruit and flowers to heroic explorers; from prize cattle to cricket matches. No book or exhibition on nineteenth century Australian art has previously brought together so many different types of subject. As a result, *The Colonial Image* should both surprise and impress on account of the variety and quality of colonial painting.

To Claire

Contents

9 Introduction
12 John Lewin
14 Joseph Lycett
16 Augustus Earle
22 Thomas Bock
24 Thomas Griffiths Wainewright
26 John Glover
30 Benjamin Duterrau
34 Mary Morton Allport
36 W.B. Gould
38 Conrad Martens
44 John Skinner Prout
46 William Duke
48 S.T. Gill
52 John Michael Crossland
54 Alexander Schramm
56 Charles Hill
58 Harden S. Melville
60 Thomas Baines
62 Robert Dowling
66 William Strutt
72 Eugene von Guérard
80 Nicholas Chevalier
82 George Rowe
84 Thomas Clark
86 Henry Gritten
88 William Dexter
90 Henry Short
92 Louis Buvelot
96 William Ford
98 Emma Minnie Boyd
100 Louis Tannert
102 Frederick Woodhouse
104 Thomas Flintoff
106 H.J. Johnstone
108 W.C. Piguenit
110 Bibliography

Robert Dowling
**Mrs Adolphus Sceales with Black Jimmie on
    Merrang Station** 1856 (detail)
oil on canvas, mounted on plywood
76.0 × 101.5 cm
Australian National Gallery

Introduction

Throughout the colonial period, professional artists in Australia were tightly constrained by the relatively small market for their work. Probably only John Glover was sufficiently wealthy to be independent of the market. Few artists were so committed to particular subjects that they painted them regardless of whether or not they would sell. Consequently, in choosing subjects for their paintings most artists either worked to commissions or sought to anticipate the 'taste' of their patrons. In some cases this prevented their executing the paintings of their choice; early in the century, particularly, artists trained in one type of painting frequently had to take up a different or wider range of painting.

Because the dominant taste of both private collectors and the various colonial 'National Galleries' was for imported European works, the settlers who purchased the work of local artists formed only a small part of the Australian art market. Generally they bought colonial paintings because they wanted Australian subjects which European artists could not produce. Occasionally, because of price or availability, they bought paintings by colonial artists of European subjects — particularly landscapes and still lifes.

In buying the work of local artists, the primary concern of the settlers was to obtain records of their achievements in the colonies and the environment in which they had been successful. To paraphrase a review of the Sydney fine arts exhibition in 1847, they wanted paintings of themselves, their homes, their ships or their animals. They also wanted paintings of their broader Australian context — especially landscapes, but also natural history paintings, pictures of Aboriginals and small scenes recording everyday life in the colonies.

Until the 1850s, colonists frequently commissioned portraits as both likenesses and documents of their success and status. Photography, invented in 1839 and widely used from the 1850s, could not compete with paintings as an expression of status since early photographs were generally small and monotone (unless hand-coloured). They were, however, cheap, they could be easily produced in multiples and they also had the attraction of a new invention which soon became highly fashionable. Because of this competition, the number of commissions for small portraits and miniatures, which generally served only as likenesses, declined significantly from the 1850s. Possibly because prices for even quite large portraits appear to have been very low, portraiture stopped attracting leading colonial artists.

Although quite highly regarded in their day, many portraits of colonists now have little appeal. Generally depicting half-length figures in their finery, at a slight angle against plain backgrounds, they are distinguished more by the attractiveness of the sitter than by the competence of the artist. More interesting are those portraits with unusual compositions or subjects, whether it be explorers in their 'bush' clothing or children with their pets or dolls. Particularly interesting are the relatively few group portraits because of the relationship between the figures, their settings, either outdoors or indoors, and their compositional complexity.

Like portraits of the colonists, paintings of animals, houses and ships were mostly documents of success, commissioned by people who wanted to celebrate their possessions in art. Notwithstanding their role as 'mere' records of property, these pictures were generally accepted without demur in the colonial period as an aspect of local painting which warranted a place in exhibitions and comment in reviews. 'Animal portraits' were usually judged in terms of the accuracy of the likeness; 'house portraits' were assessed more in terms of their compositional interest and, measured against other types of landscape, were not surprisingly sometimes found wanting.

Over the past century there have been considerable fluctuations in regard for these paintings of property. Having fallen initially into general low regard because they were thought to lack artistic interest, they have now been reassessed not only because of the charm of their sometimes naive execution and their considerable value as historical documents, but also because they formed an integral part of colonial painting. That this was the case is particularly clear with house portraits, which made up a significant part of the oeuvre and livelihood of a number of the leading colonial artists and consequently need to be taken into account in assessing the work of these men.

Particularly in the hands of John Glover and Eugene von Guérard, colonial landscape painting obtained a symbolic dimension manifestly absent from paintings of property and most portraits. For the purchasers of colonial landscapes, however, these paintings were important principally as records of the place where they had lived and flourished. Just as house portraits celebrated personal achievement in a very direct fashion — typically depicting the lavish houses built by wealthy colonists — so city views celebrated social progress and showed more generally the setting where individual colonists had succeeded. Paintings of mountains, waterfalls, fern gullies and forests were primarily exercises in the Romantic, although by showing the wilderness intact they also emphasised, through contrast, the settlers' success in establishing European civilisation in

Australia. Paintings of the settled, familiar countryside showed in a different, mundane way that Australia had been tamed and that even the commonplace in the landscape was valuable.

Because of the considerable demand for paintings of these diverse aspects of Australian scenery and the appeal of rendering 'new, undepicted' nature, landscape attracted many of the best colonial artists. Just as it evolved in Europe and North America from a relatively minor art form in the eighteenth century to a major, if not the dominant type of painting in the nineteenth century, so in Australia landscape gradually gained contemporary recognition as the most important category of colonial painting. From the mid-1850s, landscapes regularly dominated exhibitions held in Melbourne, then the art capital of Australia. Moreover, those critics who looked for the emergence of a distinctive school of Australian art pinned their hopes on landscape, both because this was the province of the leading artists and because they felt that Australia's novel scenery might engender a distinctive type of painting.

This pre-eminence of landscape within colonial painting continues, bolstered recently by a growing appreciation of the work of John Glover and Eugene von Guérard, whose paintings stand out not only because of their fine rendering of Australian scenery. While Glover took advantage of his independence from the local market to develop the most autobiographical vision of life in Australia, von Guérard painted a series of wilderness subjects which are the high point of Romanticism in colonial art. More generally, colonial landscapes retain their importance because of their dual role, however inconsistent, as documents of how Australia appeared and the type of painting in which one can most easily discern the response of both colonial artists and their patrons to their 'new' country.

Both natural history subjects and paintings of Aboriginals sometimes filled a role similar to landscape as records of the place where the colonists had lived. Much more than landscape, however, natural history painting tended towards the scientific, recording Australia's novel flora and fauna. Some pictures of Aboriginals were similarly intended as ethnographic documents, depicting the Aboriginals' appearance and 'occupations and amusements' in their 'natural' condition. Otherwise they generally ignored the European destruction of Aboriginal society, presenting a rose-tinted view of how colonisation had affected the Aboriginal people.

In rare cases, even still lifes probably served as records of Australia. The titles and contemporary descriptions of some paintings now lost — especially a number of Henry Short's fruit and flower pieces — suggest that local content may have made them emblematic of the colonies. However, the colonial content of still lifes was often insufficiently pronounced to give these paintings a manifestly Australian flavour. Numerous colonial still lifes were composed entirely of European fruit, flowers and game which probably appealed to settlers nostalgic for things at 'home'; in an effort to 'improve' Australia many colonists worked hard to acclimatise these exotics to Australian conditions.

The paintings most obviously absent from colonial art are the various types of figure composition. Colonial artists not only executed few history paintings, which were conventionally regarded as the highest form of painting because of their capacity to improve or inspire through depiction of significant events, especially those involving national valour. They also painted few religious subjects, literary pictures and large-scale 'genre' pictures showing scenes from everyday life, which are generally regarded as most typical of British painting of the Victorian era.

As noted by the Melbourne critic, James Smith, colonial artists may have attempted few history paintings partly because of 'a very general disbelief in the sufficiency of any artists we have among us to undertake such performances'. However, the principal reason for the dearth of history paintings was the lack of patrons interested in such subjects. History paintings were, almost by definition, large pictures, and regardless of the type of painting there was only a very small colonial market for big canvases. The colonists also lacked the nationalistic fervour which, until the mid-nineteenth century, created a considerable market for history paintings in Europe, and in mid-century saw history painting flourish in the United States.

A further problem for colonial history painters was the apparent shortage of appropriate events to form the subject of Australian paintings of this type. George Augustus Robinson, presented as the hero of Australia's first history paintings because of his successful conciliation of the Tasmanian Aboriginals, was regarded by many as 'a booby, seeking fame, and even notoriety by telling the black men not to break any of the ten commandments'. Burke and Wills, whose tragic deaths inspired the greatest number of colonial history paintings, were universally admired for their successful crossing of the Australian continent, but there were many colonists who doubted Burke's competence to lead an exploring expedition.

Within this context Benjamin Duterrau, the first artist committed to history painting, found no market in Hobart in the 1830s and 1840s for his pictures of

Robinson. In the following decade William Strutt, who had all the academic training to enable him to execute large, complex figure subjects, was repeatedly frustrated in his plans to find patrons for history paintings in Melbourne. 'Scantily rewarded and imperfectly appreciated', he returned to England in 1862 where he attempted a small number of colonial history subjects but, with one exception, struggled to find purchasers for these paintings.

The similar dearth of religious, literary and large genre subjects may have also been partly due to colonial artists' lack of relevant training. More important, however, was the limited market for these types of painting and competition from imported pictures. When the English portrait and subject painter, Marshall Claxton, came out to Sydney in 1851 with a large collection of figure paintings — ranging from the The Entombment of our Saviour to a nude Lady Godiva — he obtained many portrait commissions but failed to sell the larger pictures he had imported, and found little enthusiasm for figure paintings of Australian subjects. As a result, Claxton left Sydney in 1854 for 'uncivilized India' where he reportedly 'sold all his large pictures to wealthy Nabobs'.

Whereas ambitious figure painters such as Claxton and Strutt clearly had good reason for despairing over the settlers' patronage of art, from mid-century there was a considerable colonial market for small, cheap paintings — generally watercolours — of contemporary life and topical events. While a number of colonial artists worked at this type of painting, by far its finest exponent was S.T. Gill. In addition to his many animal pictures, house portraits, city views and wilderness subjects, Gill painted a wide variety of everyday scenes, especially of the life of stockmen and shepherds, and diggers on the goldfields. Although probably often painted as speculations, Gill was clearly successful with these genre pictures as he frequently painted several versions of the same subject.

With his wide-ranging talent and willingness to respond to the colonial market, Gill probably painted a greater array of subjects than any other colonial artist. His success in Adelaide, Melbourne and Sydney over a long colonial career is indicative of the way in which colonial artists could attract considerable patronage so long as they did not seek to improve their audience through narrative. In satisfying this market, colonial artists reinforced the status of their patrons, decorated their homes and gave them mementos of where they had lived. The result was the rich diversity of subjects brought together in this book.

John Lewin
1770-1819

When John Lewin arrived in New South Wales in 1800, he was the first professional artist to come to Australia independently of an exploring expedition. Born into a family of ornithologists and artists, Lewin was attracted to Australia as a field for art and science. His primary intention in coming to New South Wales was to collect natural history specimens and draw them for publication.

During Lewin's first years in Australia, when he lived at Parramatta, he worked mainly at his profession as a natural history artist. Apart from painting a wide range of Australian flora and fauna, he succeeded in publishing two illustrated scientific books on butterflies and birds. However, probably because of a limited demand for his natural history subjects, Lewin moved to Sydney in 1808 where he painted a much broader range of subjects, including portraits and landscapes. In 1815 he became the first professional artist to travel to the Australian interior

when he accompanied Governor Macquarie across the Blue Mountains to Bathurst.

Lewin's finest Australian paintings are the large presentation drawings of natural history subjects which he executed for prominent colonists. He painted both botanical subjects — generally against plain backgrounds — and zoological subjects, sometimes in landscape settings as with *The variegated lizard* (or the giant tree goanna) he painted for Governor Bligh in 1807. Although Lewin received little remuneration for his work, these pictures were highly valued by his patrons. Writing in 1814, the Sydney merchant Alexander Riley noted:

> I have had a pair of the most elegant Flowers painted by Mr Lewen [sic], viz the Gigantic Lily and the Waratah done in his good style ... I may with truth repeat the remark of all who have seen them, viz 'That they are worthy the Palace of a Prince' ... Lewen has charged me £12/12/-, and from his high style of finishing them he did not earn journeyman's wages.

J.W. Lewin
The variegated lizard of New South Wales 1807
watercolour
26.2 × 45.2 cm
private collection

J.W. Lewin
The gigantic lyllie of New South Wales 1810
watercolour
54.0 × 43.2 cm
Art Gallery of New South Wales

Joseph Lycett

1774-1827

Joseph Lycett was one of a large number of convict artists who worked in Australia in the late eighteenth and first half of the nineteenth centuries. Like Lycett, most of these artists had received only limited training and had achieved no prominence in England. Many of these men also took up very different types of art in Australia to that which they had practised in England. Lycett had been a painter of portraits and miniatures in England. In Australia he worked principally at landscape painting. Similarly, Thomas Bock had been an engraver in Birmingham, but in Hobart became a portrait painter.

Born in Staffordshire, Lycett was sentenced in 1811 to fourteen years' transportation for having uttered forged notes. Shortly after his arrival in Sydney in 1814 he gained his ticket-of-leave, but in 1815 recommitted his original offence and consequently was sent to Newcastle, the colony's place of secondary punishment. There he worked as architect and artist for the settlement's commander, Captain James Wallis, until he received a conditional pardon in 1818.

Over the next four years Lycett painted numerous botanical studies in addition to the landscape paintings which form the bulk of his work. He made a number of sketching expeditions around Sydney but probably did not go further afield. His more distant New South Wales subjects, and all his Tasmanian views, appear to have been based on sketches by other artists.

On returning to England in 1822 with an absolute pardon, Lycett continued this line of work, which culminated in his major series of aquatints, *Views in Australia* (1824-25). Following its publication, Lycett hoped to produce a companion volume on Australian natural history, but he died in 1827. (In any event, the second book would probably not have been published as the *Views* were not a success, and were remaindered in 1830.)

Lycett's colonial landscapes range from wilderness views to cityscapes. To quote the advertisement for his *Views*, he showed that Australia had 'scenes of natural grandeur, beauty, richness, and variety' which could

Joseph Lycett
View on the Macquarie River near the ford, on the road to Launceston c. 1824
watercolour
17.8 × 28.0 cm
Australian National Gallery

not be contemplated 'without impressions of mingled delight and wonder at such magnificent specimens of the stupendous power of Nature ... in all the freshness of a new Creation!' He also depicted the success of the settlers in establishing European civilisation in Australia:

> The gloomy grandeur of solitary woods and forests exchanged for the noise and bustle of thronged marts of commerce; while the dens of savage animals, and the hiding places of yet more savage men, have become transformed into peaceful villages or cheerful towns.

Lastly, he showed the potential of the colonies for further investment and development.

In recording the success of the settlers in converting the colonial wilderness, Lycett painted a number of views of the houses and farms established by the colonists in and around Sydney. The dwellings selected by him range from elegant harbourside villas to the rather rudimentary manager's house on Raby, Alexander Riley's farm of 1,215 hectares near Liverpool. In 1820, about the time Lycett is most likely to have visited, Raby was one of the most important sheep properties in New South Wales. Although depicting a relatively primitive house, Lycett's painting reveals most graphically the 'industry of man' through the contrast between the cleared pasture and the surrounding screen of eucalypts.

Most of Lycett's landscapes presenting Australia as a field for investment and development are of Tasmania. In these paintings, such as *View on the Macquarie River*, Lycett generally depicted fine pasture land unoccupied by livestock. As described in Lycett's book of *Views* this painting shows

> . . . one of the most luxuriant and extensive plains in the Colony of Van Diemen's Land, called Argyle Plains. This tract of land consists of a fine dark loamy clay; it is remarkably free from timber, and is well watered at all seasons of the year.

The painting clearly demonstrates the colony's pastoral potential and seems to invite prospective settlers to bring their flocks and herds to the well-grassed plains.

Joseph Lycett
The homestead at Raby c. 1824
watercolour
17.8 × 28.0 cm
Australian National Gallery

Augustus Earle

1793-1838

Augustus Earle was the first freelance professional artist to tour the world. Born in London, Earle exhibited banditti subjects at the Royal Academy between 1808 and 1815, and then set out on his artistic travels. After two years working around the Mediterranean he went to the United States in 1818 and South America in 1820. Four years later, en route to India, Earle was accidentally abandoned on the small South Atlantic island of Tristan da Cunha, where he remained for eight months until rescued by a ship bound for Tasmania. He arrived in Hobart in January 1825 and reached Sydney in the middle of the year. Apart from seven months in New Zealand, he remained in New South Wales until October 1828 when he left for London.

In the course of his extensive travels, Earle primarily painted watercolours of views and local customs. In New South Wales he continued this practice, especially on the two major sketching trips he made from Sydney — first to the Blue Mountains at the end of 1826 and then to the Illawarra district in May 1827. He probably hoped to find a market in Sydney for works based on his sketches, but there appears to have been little interest in these subjects. As a result, he painted few, if any, oil paintings of colonial scenery until his return to England. Because his lithographed *Views in Australia* found few purchasers in Sydney in 1826, Earle was forced to discontinue publication after only two parts had appeared.

Earle's main income as an artist in New South Wales came from portraiture. While he lived in Sydney he was the only artist to paint large-scale portraits in oils, and he consequently gained many portrait commissions from prominent colonists. Otherwise, Earle supported himself by selling artist's materials, books, engravings and concert tickets, by printing circulars on his lithographic press and by taking pupils.

One of Earle's first portraits in Sydney was of Sir Thomas Brisbane (1773-1860), the retiring Governor of New South Wales. Brisbane was a close friend of Earle's half-brother, Captain (later Admiral) Smyth, and this connection with the governor probably helped Earle obtain his many portrait commissions in Sydney. When Earle's *Views in New South Wales and Van Diemen's Land* was published in London in 1830, he dedicated the book to Brisbane.

Earle was commissioned to paint Brisbane by the Civil Officers — that is, the civil servants — of the New South Wales Government, which makes the portrait the first official colonial painting to be publicly commissioned in Australia. At a meeting at Government House in November 1825 the officers decided to commission Brisbane's portrait from a local rather than an English artist

> ... on account of the risks and delay attending the transmission of one from Europe, and with a view to combine a resemblance of His Excellency with a monument of the progress of the fine arts in New South Wales, under His Excellency's administration.

The officers probably also commissioned Earle because his portraits were relatively inexpensive. As a Sydney newspaper noted, 'If an *inferior* artist in England had had the job, it would have cost about 200 l. Mr Earl, in Sydney, (where everything else is paid with 200 l. per cent) receives 50 l.'

The resulting picture of Brisbane was one of Earle's most ambitious and successful portraits — despite his characteristic awkwardness in the articulation of the figure and the clothing. Wearing blue 'undress' civilian court dress and the insignia of Knight Commander of the Bath, Brisbane stands at a table, in front of a view of Sydney Heads. Contemporary critics judged the portrait 'a very fine picture', and a 'happy', even a 'capital' or 'striking', likeness.

The only other full-length portraits executed by Earle in Sydney were commissioned by Captain John Piper (1773-1851), who first came out to Sydney in 1792 as an ensign in the newly formed New South Wales Corp. From 1814 Piper held the highly remunerative post of Naval Officer, with responsibility for customs, excise and harbour dues. By 1825, when he reached the height of his career and probably commissioned the paintings from Earle, Piper was one of the wealthiest colonists in Sydney. In one painting Earle showed Piper standing beneath a decorative eucalyptus tree, with a backdrop of his official residence, Henrietta Villa, on what is now known as Point Piper. The other painting depicts Piper's wife, Mary Anne Shears (c. 1795-1871), the daughter of a convict, together with four of their children in one of the domed rooms of Henrietta Villa.

Earle also painted two smaller portraits of Captain and Mrs Piper, that of Captain Piper being typical of Earle's Sydney portraits. The picture is simply of head and shoulders, depicting Captain Piper at a slight angle. That of Mrs Piper, however, is more unusual in the stark simplicity of the frontal pose and the way in which her face is crowded by the framing edge. On account of the Pipers' dissimilar poses and the different backgrounds against which the two figures are set, it is likely that the two portraits were not painted as a pair.

Between his many portrait commissions, Earle chose to paint Bungaree, the most famous Australian Aboriginal of the early nineteenth century and,

Augustus Earle
Sir Thomas Brisbane 1825–26
oil on canvas
221.0 × 114.8 cm
Government House, Sydney

Augustus Earle
Mrs John Piper c.1825–26
oil on cardboard on wood panel
45.8 × 31.0 cm
Australian National Gallery

consistent with this status, one of the Aboriginals most frequently portrayed in colonial art. Apart from the painting and two lithographs by Earle, he was the subject of three lithographs by other artists issued posthumously, perhaps the clearest indication of Bungaree's renown.

Bungaree, who came from the Broken Bay area, gained his fame partly through his assistance to the colonists and partly on account of his leadership of the township Aboriginals in Sydney until his death in 1830. He accompanied three naval expeditions in

Australia, including Flinders' circumnavigation of the continent in 1801-02 and P.P. King's voyage to north-west Australia in 1817. As a reward for his services, various governors and colonels gave Bungaree discarded uniforms and a cocked hat. In 1815 Governor Macquarie decorated Bungaree with a brass plate inscribed 'Bungaree: King of the Blacks', a completely fictitious title as Bungaree had no tribal authority.

In his portrait, Earle showed Bungaree engaged in the activity for which he was best known: welcoming strangers to the colony, whom he then characteristically informed that the land was 'his'. As described by Earle, he is making 'the graceful bow ... [which] he copied from one of the Governors, and those who recollect the original, say it is exact'. In

Augustus Earle
Captain John Piper c. 1825–26
oil on canvas
44.4 × 30.8 cm
Australian National Gallery

certain respects, the portrait therefore appears as a counterpart to Earle's portrait of Sir Thomas Brisbane since it shows Bungaree dressed and acting as if he were governor.

Following his return to England, Earle painted a small number of oil paintings of Australian scenery, including *A bivouac of travellers in Australia* which he showed at the Royal Academy in 1838, just a few months before his death. The painting, based on sketches made by Earle in 1827, is one of numerous works by colonial artists to celebrate the dense subtropical vegetation of the Illawarra district. At the

same time, the picture gives a sense of the spirit of adventure which Earle clearly felt on his Australian expeditions. As he described in a letter of doggerel verse written in 1827:

Thro' Liverpool and Campbelltown — a western course
  we keep
But then our heads, we southward turn — and steer
  towards the deep
Now Bumberry curren's pleasant vales — and Appin's
  plains are past
And Illawarra Mountain steep — we've got safe o'er at
  last
We traversed Mountain Bog and Bush — and
  Bivouaked at night
Determined hunger and fatigue — we'd turn into delight
It was a curious sight to see — us laying round our fire
Our [teaster] Heaven's Canopy — our down bed on the
  brier.

Augustus Earle
Bungaree, a native of New South Wales c. 1826
oil on canvas
69.0 × 50.9 cm
Rex Nan Kivell Collection, National Library of Australia

Augustus Earle
**A bivouac of travellers in Australia in a cabbage tree
 forest, day break** c. 1838
oil on canvas
118.1 × 81.9 cm
Rex Nan Kivell Collection, National Library of Australia

Thomas Bock

1790-1855

Thomas Bock was the leading portrait painter in Hobart from the mid-1820s until his death in 1855. Born in England at Hammerwich near Lichfield, Bock worked as an engraver and miniature painter in Birmingham from at least 1815. Eight years later, he was convicted for 'Administering Drugs to procure Abortion to a young Woman named Ann Yates' whom Bock, a married man and father of four legitimate children, had apparently seduced. As a result, he was transported to Tasmania in 1824.

From the time of his arrival in Hobart, Bock worked as an artist even though he only received his conditional pardon in 1832 and free pardon in 1833. He worked primarily as a portrait painter, receiving numerous commissions. Generally, he painted successful colonists and their families, such as Jessie Robertson (1835-49), eldest daughter of William Robertson, a wealthy Hobart merchant and holder of extensive pastoral land in Victoria. However Bock also executed numerous small portraits of 'domesticated'

Aboriginals including the 'last' Tasmanian Aboriginal, Truganini, and Manalargenna. Between 1830 and 1834 these Aboriginals accompanied the Methodist bricklayer, George Augustus Robinson, on his expeditions through Tasmania during which he 'conciliated' the remaining 'wild' Tasmanian Aboriginals and peacefully brought them into Hobart for transportation to Flinders Island.

In 1832 Robinson commissioned Bock to paint a series of portraits of these Aboriginals and, over the following decade, a number of other colonists followed suit. They may have done so partly because of the role of the Aboriginals in assisting the colonists (just as mainland Aboriginals who accompanied explorers were the subject of popular lithographs). However, the principal motive for Bock's commission was probably the desire for accurate ethnographic records, prompted by the belief that the Tasmanian Aboriginals would soon be extinct.

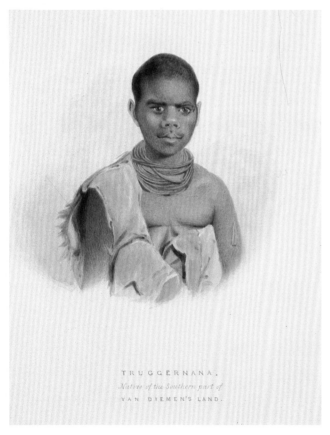

Thomas Bock
Truganini 1837
watercolour
29.2 × 22.0 cm
Tasmanian Museum and Art Gallery

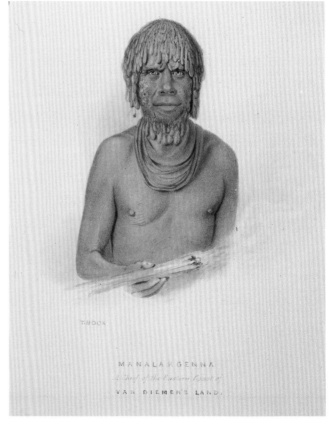

Thomas Bock
Manalargenna c. 1834–35
watercolour
26.5 × 18.3 cm
Royal Anthropological Institute of Great Britain and
    Ireland (on loan to the Australian National Gallery)

Thomas Bock
Jessie Robertson c. 1847
oil on canvas
76.2 × 63.5 cm
private collection

Thomas Griffiths Wainewright

1794-1847

Of all convict artists, Thomas Griffiths Wainewright was by far the best trained and connected. Born in Richmond, London, he studied painting under the Royal Academicians John Linnell and Thomas Phillips, and regularly exhibited at the Royal Academy in the 1820s where his subject pictures echoed the pre-Romantic style of Henry Fuseli. He also wrote art criticism and essays for literary magazines like *Blackwood's* and the *London Magazine*, and became part of the literary circle around the essayist and critic, Charles Lamb.

Wainewright fell from society as a result of living beyond his means. In the first half of the 1820s he forged a power of attorney to get access to his inheritance which he had placed in trust for his wife. Because of the deaths in rapid succession of his uncle, mother-in-law and sister-in-law around 1830, he was also suspected of poisoning his relatives to gain access to their estates. There is no firm evidence that Wainewright was responsible for these deaths and, indeed, no charges were ever laid. However, as a result of his forgery of the power of attorney he was convicted in 1837 of attempting to defraud the Bank of England and was transported to Tasmania.

As a convict artist in Hobart, Wainewright was forced to abandon his large oil paintings of literary subjects for modest-sized pencil, watercolour and crayon portraits. His work was as accomplished as that of his fellow convict, Thomas Bock, but his colonial oeuvre was much smaller — partly because of ill-health and partly because, unlike Bock, he had little opportunity to work as an artist while a convict. Until about 1840 Wainewright worked on the roads in a chain-gang; from then until 1845 he was first a wardsman and then a patient at the Hobart Hospital.

Prior to gaining his ticket-of-leave in December 1845, Wainewright generally executed portraits for people who formed part of his immediate world as a convict, such as James Cutmear, who from 1840 was Gatekeeper at the Prisoners' Barracks where Wainewright was an inmate until 1842. Some of these pictures were undoubtedly commissions, but others were probably painted by Wainewright in gratitude for acts of kindness. It was only in the last two years of his life, when Wainewright was first allowed to live in Hobart and then granted a conditional pardon, that he worked for the Tasmanian population at large.

Thomas Griffiths Wainewright
The Cutmear twins c. 1842
watercolour
32.4 × 30.0 cm
Australian National Gallery

John Glover

1767-1849

John Glover was the only colonial artist to have achieved a considerable reputation in Europe before choosing to settle in Australia. Working in the style of the seventeenth-century landscape painter, Claude Lorrain, Glover was one of the most successful watercolour painters in England in the early nineteenth century, and was President of the Old Water-Colour Society during 1807-08. From about 1817 he began to work increasingly in oils; from 1820 to 1825 he held annual exhibitions of his work in London, and in 1823 was a founding member of the Society of British Artists, with whom he subsequently exhibited.

By the time Glover emigrated to Tasmania in 1830, changes in taste had reduced the market for his work from its heights of the early nineteenth century. However, this decline in Glover's artistic fortune was hardly reason for him to leave England, since he had accumulated considerable wealth. Aged sixty-three, Glover went to Tasmania because three of his sons had already emigrated. He looked forward to being a substantial landowner in the colony and painting its novel scenery. He was 'delighted' by 'the expectation of finding a beautiful new world — new landscapes, new trees, new flowers, new animals, birds, etc'.

Following his arrival in Tasmania in March 1831, Glover bought a farm at Tea Tree Brush near Brighton, north of Hobart, but lived in a house in the city where he painted only few pictures. Then, in March 1832, he settled on a property he called Patterdale, at Mills Plains at the foot of Ben Lomond east of Launceston. Unlike other colonial artists Glover was able to make this move to country living because Australian patronage was of only minor importance to him. He was sufficiently wealthy that he did not need

John Glover
The Island of Madiera begun 1831, completed 1839
oil on canvas
51.0 × 72.0 cm
Australian National Gallery

John Glover
Patterdale landscape with rainbow c. 1835
watercolour 21.0 × 32.4 cm
Australian National Gallery

John Glover
My Harvest Home 1835
oil on canvas 76.2 × 114.0 cm
Tasmanian Museum and Art Gallery

John Glover
A corroboree of natives in Mills Plains 1832–33
oil on canvas   56.5 × 71.4 cm
Art Gallery of South Australia

to live off his art and, in any event, the market he wanted to exploit and impress was at 'home' in England.

After initially painting little at Patterdale because of the upheaval of moving, Glover's output during 1833-35 became prolific, as it had been in England. During 1835-36 he sent almost one hundred oil paintings to London, sixty of which were shown in a one-man exhibition of Glover's work held in mid-1835.

Perhaps the most striking aspect of Glover's Australian work is its autobiographical element. Although there is a strong personal element in the work of some amateur colonial artists, the work of professional artists is generally anonymous in the sense that it records other people's land and other people's lives. Glover's freedom from the colonial market allowed him repeatedly to paint his own landscape at Patterdale and events in his own life which were important to him.

He began to emphasise the autobiographical on leaving England. Already on the voyage out to

Australia on the barque, *Thomas Laurie*, he began *The Island of Madiera* which depicts the *Thomas Laurie* with a fishing party off the Portuguese North Atlantic island of Madiera. Following his arrival in Tasmania, he painted *Hobart Town, taken from the artist's garden*, rather than the standard, impersonal view of Hobart seen across the Derwent with Mount Wellington as a backdrop (see p. 87). He also painted *A view of the first farm purchased by the artist fifteen miles from Hobart Town, near Brighton*.

The personal is most apparent, however, in Glover's many paintings of his property, Patterdale, which was his favourite subject while in Tasmania. As the son of a small Leicestershire farmer, Glover appears to have derived great satisfaction from being a substantial landholder in Tasmania, and he probably gained unusual enjoyment from recording his own farm on canvas. For Glover's English patrons it was immaterial whose property he depicted, while for Glover it was, of course, easiest to sketch his own land.

In his paintings of Patterdale and Mills Plains, such as *Patterdale landscape with rainbow*, Glover provided the first extensive series of views of Australia as a 'pastoral Arcadia'. These paintings are Arcadian in their sense of ease and plenitude and their concealment of the hardships faced by the early

John Glover
**Castles in Italy near Otricoli: a Brown Friar and a
 thief being taken to prison** 1841
oil on canvas 78.6 × 114.6 cm
Australian National Gallery

settlers. They are 'pastoral', not in the conventional
sense of works depicting an imagined Golden Age as
described in the poetry of Virgil and Ovid, but rather
because they show Australia as a land of sheep or,
more usually, cattle.

Glover's painting, *My Harvest Home*, which he
inscribed '... begun March 19th 1835 the day the
harvest was all got in', is exceptional in colonial art not
only for depicting the settlers' attempts at agriculture,
but also for showing them actively engaged in manual
labour. Yet with the successful completion of the
harvest imminent, the men in *My Harvest Home*
appear untroubled by the arduousness of their
employment and the scene is characterised by a
profound sense of physical well-being. In a letter of
July 1839, John Glover junior wrote:

> We sow, plant, fence and break up new ground in
> progressive order and our crops thank goodness turn
> out equal to most, our wheat in particular often
> surpasses most of our neighbours.

Glover also painted several Arcadian landscapes
around Patterdale in which he replaced the sheep and
cattle, which actually occupied most of the land, with
the Aboriginals who were its former inhabitants. In
these paintings Glover ignored the destruction of the

Tasmanian Aboriginal population by the settlers.
Instead, probably prompted by the belief that the
Tasmanians would soon be extinct, he sought with
some concern for ethnographic accuracy 'to give an
idea of the gay, happy life the natives led before the
White people came here ...'. Although giving no
indication of the appearance of the Aboriginals, *A
corroboree of natives in Mills Plains* is consistent with
an early account that: 'The native dances of the east
... consist principally of performing a circle round the
fire, striking the ground with one hand and then
jumping up . . .' Of another of his paintings of
corroborees, Glover wrote: 'I have seen more
enjoyment and mirth on such occasions than I ever
saw in a Ball Room in England.'

Like many later colonial landscape painters, Glover
also painted a number of European subjects while in
Australia. Early in his Tasmanian career he painted
these pictures for his English audience; later he
painted them for his own pleasure as well as for
colonists who were homesick for Europe. Remarkably,
given this nostalgic aspect of these pictures, the
landscape — though based on sketches made in
Europe — frequently takes on a Tasmanian quality.
This is true of one of Glover's last oil paintings,
Castles in Italy near Otricoli, which depicts part of
Umbria visited by Glover in 1818. Completed by
Glover nearly twenty-three years later, on his seventy-
fourth birthday in 1841, the trees have something of
the openness of eucalypts and the hills have the
blondness of many of Glover's Tasmanian landscapes.

Benjamin Duterrau

1767-1851

Together with John Glover, Benjamin Duterrau was one of a small group of artists who chose to come to Australia very late in their careers. Unlike Glover, Duterrau had been a minor artist in England, exhibiting only a small number of portraits and genre pieces in London. Originally he intended to emigrate to Tasmania to work as drawing master and music teacher at a school in Hobart, but this position was filled by another artist, Henry Mundy. Nevertheless, possibly influenced by the well-publicised example of Glover who had set out for Tasmania in 1830 aged sixty-three, Duterrau emigrated in 1832 when sixty-five years old.

Over the ten-year period during which he was active as an artist in Hobart, Duterrau made a major contribution to colonial art. He was responsible for the first etchings executed in Australia, he made some of the first sculptures, and gave the first recorded lecture on art in Australia. However, Duterrau is most important for his numerous oil paintings of Tasmanian Aboriginals. In addition to two series of portraits of the Tasmanians, he executed a number of paintings of their 'occupations and amusements'. Most significantly, he executed the first Australian history paintings — a series of pictures recording the 'conciliation' of the Tasmanians by the Methodist bricklayer, George Augustus Robinson. Except for his first four portraits of Aboriginals (which were eventually bought by the Colonial Government in 1837 in response to a public petition), Duterrau found no

Benjamin Duterrau
Native taking a kangaroo 1837
oil on canvas
121.5 × 167.5 cm
Australian National Gallery

Benjamin Duterrau
Native taking a kangaroo 1837 (detail)
oil on canvas
121.5 × 167.5 cm
Australian National Gallery

Benjamin Duterrau
Mr Robinson's first interview with Timmy 1840
oil on canvas
113.0 × 142.0 cm
Australian National Gallery

market for his paintings of Aboriginals. Yet he persevered with these paintings because of his interest in the Aboriginals and in Robinson's achievements.

Although Duterrau is known to have painted a number of very large pictures of the Tasmanians' methods of hunting and corroborees, only one of these paintings, *Native taking a kangaroo* (1837), has been located. This painting is unique among known colonial paintings in its attempt to capture an individual likeness while recording the 'occupations' of Aboriginals in a painting close to life-size. The size of the work, the medium used, the triangular composition and the pose of the Aboriginal (based on Antique sculpture) all indicate that in *Native taking a kangaroo* Duterrau was endeavouring to elevate ethnographic illustration to the status of high art.

Insofar as can be determined, *Native taking a kangaroo* is a broadly accurate record of one of the methods used by the Aboriginals in the 1830s to hunt kangaroos. Prior to the arrival of Europeans in Tasmania, there were no dogs on the island and the Aboriginals hunted kangaroos with spears, running down the wounded animals. However, after dogs were introduced into Tasmania, the Aboriginals used them to chase kangaroos until they were worn out. Then — as appears imminent in Duterrau's painting — the Aboriginals killed the kangaroos by beating them on the head (rather than spearing them).

Duterrau's painting departs from ethnographic fact in two main respects. First, the double-ended pointed stick held by the Aboriginal, although described by Duterrau as a waddy or single-headed club, does not resemble this type of weapon, which would in fact probably have been used to kill kangaroos. Rather, it is a throwing-stick of a type peculiar to Tasmania. Second, although the Aboriginals sometimes wore kangaroo skins on their shoulders as cloaks, they did not conform to the nineteenth century European

Benjamin Duterrau
The Conciliation 1840
oil on canvas
119.0 × 168.0 cm
Tasmanian Museum and Art Gallery

convention of modesty by wearing loin cloths.

Duterrau's paintings, *The Conciliation* and *Mr Robinson's first interview with Timmy*, both show George Augustus Robinson dressed in his 'bush hat', 'conciliating' the 'wild' Tasmanian Aboriginals with the help of his 'domesticated' followers. These history paintings were conceived by Duterrau in 1834 as a tribute to Robinson's success in peacefully persuading the Tasmanians to surrender. Because of the marked contrast between Robinson's 'friendly mission' and the settlers' failure to subjugate the Aboriginals by force, many colonists including Duterrau came to look on Robinson with great admiration. Duterrau therefore hoped to find public support for his history paintings celebrating Robinson's work. However, after waiting six years without attracting patronage, he executed his paintings, almost certainly in the knowledge that they would not sell.

By 1840, when Duterrau painted his pictures of the 'conciliation', approximately half the Aboriginals who had been removed to Flinders Island as a result of Robinson's work had died, including all the Aboriginals depicted in *The Conciliation* and *Mr Robinson's first interview with Timmy*. Robinson had also left Tasmania for Victoria, and the colonists' regard for his work had declined markedly. Nevertheless, Duterrau continued to think of Robinson as the heroic missionary who induced the Aboriginals 'to quit barbarous for civilized life'. According to one visitor to Duterrau's studio in late 1841, the artist pointed to a portrait of Robinson and exclaimed: 'There is a real hero, though not one of your world's heroes.' 'With glowing face', Duterrau turned again and again towards Robinson's portrait 'and once more rehearsed his noble deeds'.

Mary Morton Allport

1806-1895

Mary Morton Allport (née Chapman) was one of numerous women artists who worked in Australia throughout the colonial period. Whereas these women were generally amateurs whose work was fairly limited in range, Allport worked as a professional artist and her subjects were remarkably diverse. As a result, she stands out as one of the most important and interesting colonial 'lady painters'.

Born in Birmingham, Allport studied art at a school run by her future mother-in-law in Staffordshire. In 1826 she married the Allport's youngest son, Joseph, and in 1831 they emigrated to Tasmania. The Allports first lived near Brighton where Joseph Allport unsuccessfully tried farming, while Mary became the first professional woman artist in Australia, obtaining commissions to paint portrait miniatures in Hobart. From late 1832 the Allports lived in Hobart where Mary continued to produce portrait miniatures, painted landscapes and natural history studies, and became the first woman to make etchings, engravings and lithographs in Australia.

Allport's painting of a waratah, *Telopea punctata, from the mountain pass above Barrett's Mill* is in one respect 'typical of her time and sex' since flowers were the subject most frequently painted by women. However, the painting is unusual in that it does not depict the waratah against the conventional, plain background. Instead, it shows the waratah in its natural setting.

Painted around 1840, the *Telopea punctata* also appears as an important mark in Allport's growing appreciation of the Australian bush. When she first arrived in Tasmania she longed for English flowers and dreamt of being given snowdrops. By the time she painted the waratah, however, she had clearly 'accepted Australian flora as beautiful rather than curious'. A decade later she wrote, 'Nothing in the world is so graceful as the Whitey-blue gums, except the English Birch and that has not the lovely colour.'

Mary Morton Allport
Telopea punctata, from the mountain pass above Barrett's Mill c. 1840
watercolour
49.0 × 38.0 cm
Allport Library and Museum of Fine Arts
State Library of Tasmania

W.B. Gould
1803-1853

William Buelow Gould was the most prolific painter of still lifes in Australia in the first half of the nineteenth century. Born in Liverpool, England, as William Holland — a name he discarded in 1826 on deserting his wife and child — Gould had some training as an artist before being transported to Tasmania in 1827 for stealing some clothes. As a convict, Gould was twice assigned to prominent colonial officials who had him paint extensive series of natural history studies of plants and fish. He also painted occasional still lifes and continued this type of work on receiving his certificate of freedom in 1835. Over the next eighteen years, apart from two further terms of imprisonment in 1845 and 1846-48 for stealing, he painted primarily fruit and flower and dead game subjects.

Gould was not a particularly accomplished painter: his portraits are fairly crude and, in his still lifes, objects such as the cherries, gooseberries and strawberries in *Cabbage roses and fruit* tend to float above the table on which they are meant to rest. Nevertheless, Gould's large output of still lifes suggests he found a substantial market for these paintings — probably in hotels and taverns in return for drink, as suggested by legend, and among the lower middle class who were the sitters for his occasional portraits.

Notwithstanding his work as a natural history artist, Gould showed little interest in Australian flora and fauna in his still lifes. Instead, most of his paintings, such as *Cabbage roses and fruit*, follow standard European models and depict European fruit, flowers and game. Although he sometimes inscribed these pictures 'painted from nature', it is likely he painted them from engravings or from memory for a public nostalgic for things European.

Gould's painting *Fish on a blue and white plate* is similarly a conventional composition, and the fly is a common addition to a still life of food. Yet the body and tail shape of the fish, the position of the fins and details of the head seem to indicate that Gould painted them from actual specimens, most likely redbait. If so, *Fish on a blue and white plate* provides an early instance of the meeting in colonial art of natural-history painting and the conventional still life form.

W.B. Gould
Cabbage roses and fruit 1851
oil on canvas
50.4 × 61.0 cm
Australian National Gallery

W.B. Gould
Fish on a blue and white plate 1845
oil on canvas
20.3 × 30.5 cm
Australian National Gallery

Conrad Martens

1801-1878

Conrad Martens was the main Australian exponent of the British school of watercolourists which, in the first decade of the nineteenth century, transformed both the technique and status of watercolour painting. Led by J. M. W. Turner and Thomas Girtin, these artists raised watercolour from a medium used mainly for small tinted drawings to an independent expressive mode of painting rivalling oil.

Martens, who studied with the popular English watercolour painter A. V. Copley Fielding, came to Australia more by chance than design. When he left England in 1833 his intention was to make a three-year cruise to India aboard the *Hyacinth*. However, en route, at Montevideo in Uruguay, he switched to the survey ship *Beagle* which, because of insufficient cabin space, took him only as far as Valparaiso, Chile. Martens then made his own way to Tahiti and New Zealand, finally reaching Sydney in April 1835.

Martens' initial intention was to stay temporarily in New South Wales and then go on to India. As a Sydney newspaper reported shortly after his arrival:

> He is wandering ... in search of the picturesque, and having culled some of the beauties of South America and other quarters, has fixed his residence, for some months ... on these shores ...

Martens soon decided to settle in New South Wales, however, where he remained until his death.

During his long career as a colonial artist, Martens made lithographs and took pupils during times of economic hardship. Generally, however, he relied on the considerable local market for landscapes. Especially during his first seven years in the colony, a period of general prosperity, he found numerous purchasers for his watercolours. As indicated by Martens' own records, probably about half of these paintings stayed in Australia while the remainder soon

Conrad Martens
View of Sydney from Neutral Bay c. 1850s
watercolour
45.1 x 65.2 cm
Australian National Gallery

Conrad Martens
View of Sydney from Neutral Bay c. 1850s (detail)
watercolour
45.1 × 65.2 cm
Australian National Gallery

Conrad Martens
The Cottage, Rose Bay 1857
watercolour
46.1 × 66.0 cm
Australian National Gallery

went to England, having been bought by either travellers, departing colonists, or settlers who wished to give their family at 'home' an impression of where they lived.

Throughout his residence in New South Wales, Sydney harbour was one of Martens' principal subjects. In most of these views, he was concerned to show the size and beauty of the harbour as well as civic progress — a point he reinforced in a number of paintings by including Aboriginals in the foreground as a contrast to the city in the background. Beginning in the 1850s, however, Martens painted a number of harbour views in which his interest shifted away from topography to a Romantic concern with light and atmosphere reflecting the influence of Turner. In a few of these paintings, including *View of Sydney from Neutral Bay*, he depicted marvellous storm-cloud effects: a marked contrast to nearly all colonial landscapes which show Australia bathed in sunshine.

Martens also obtained many commissions to paint 'house portraits', both around Sydney and in country regions. In some of these works he focused on the building. More often he set the house in a larger landscape, as in his picture of The Cottage, Rose Bay, a house designed in 1834 by the leading Sydney

architect John Verge, and built the following year for the businessman James Holt. The painting was commissioned in 1857 by The Cottage's then owner Sir Daniel Cooper, who lived at Rose Bay between 1843 and 1848 and then again during 1856-57. Cooper appears to have acquired Martens' painting as a memento of his residence at Rose Bay since in 1857 he moved to his new mansion, Woollahra House at Point Piper.

Very much as a counterpart to his house portraits, Martens painted many views of spectacular Australian scenery, especially waterfalls. These 'wilderness' pictures not only celebrate the grandeur of Australian nature but also emphasise, through contrast, the achievements of the settlers in establishing their pastoral domains and building their fine houses. In most of these paintings, Martens showed the wilderness as forbidding and hostile to man. However, in his painting of Fitzroy Falls — bought by a pastoralist, Charles Throsby, who also commissioned Martens to paint his house — Martens depicted Europeans at ease within a wilderness landscape and enjoying its splendours. While one of the two men at left on the outcrop above the waterfall stands and admires the distant view, the other, closer to the edge,

Conrad Martens
The Cottage, Rose Bay 1857 (detail)
watercolour
46.1 × 66.0 cm
Australian National Gallery

Conrad Martens
Fitzroy Falls 1836
watercolour
46.1 × 66.4 cm
The H.W.B. Chester Memorial Collection

is comfortably recumbent and seems oblivious to the
dangers around him. This image of Europeans
enjoying spectacular scenery was not a product of
Martens' fancy. His preparatory sketch of Fitzroy Falls
already includes two figures in these attitudes and it
therefore seems that in his painting Martens was
simply recording his companions on the occasion
when he went to the falls.

In the 1870s, toward the end of his career, Martens
had a late flowering, producing a number of his finest
landscapes. These late works include three paintings
of the newly built Great Zig Zag railway line near
Lithgow, where Martens went early in 1872 on his last
major sketching expedition. Colonial painters generally
chose not to paint industrial and engineering subjects.
However, like several photographers, Martens was
attracted by the railway line which was a triumph of
colonial engineering because of its sharp bends and
mastery of a very steep gradient. In his painting
Viaducts on the descent to the Lithgow Valley,
Martens ignored how the line scarred and disfigured
the country it traversed. Instead, he treated the railway
as an elegant classical structure which fitted
harmoniously into the landscape.

Conrad Martens
Viaducts on the descent to the Lithgow Valley 1872
watercolour and gouache on card
45.8 × 66.8 cm
Australian National Gallery

John Skinner Prout

1805-1876

John Skinner Prout was a nephew of Samuel Prout, the well-known English watercolourist, lithographer and teacher. A self-taught artist, Prout painted topographic watercolours and produced architectural lithographs in the west of England in the 1830s. However, toward the end of this decade he appears to have struggled financially since, after two years' 'continued difficulties and harrassment of mind', he emigrated to Sydney in 1840. Three years later Prout moved to Hobart, probably as a result of the depression which then gripped New South Wales. Four years later, having achieved considerable success in Tasmania, he decided to return to England. After being fêted at a farewell concert attended by 150 people including the Tasmanian Governor, Sir William Denison, he left Hobart in April 1848.

During his residence in Australia, Prout played a leading role as a painter, printmaker, teacher and promoter of the fine arts. Apart from painting many picturesque landscapes, he was responsible for three volumes of lithographic views — of Sydney, Tasmania, and Melbourne and Geelong. He attracted many pupils, especially in Hobart where he was responsible for turning landscape sketching into the 'prevalent fashionable epidemic' of the mid-1840s. In Sydney, Hobart and Melbourne he gave lectures on art, while in Hobart he was primarily responsible for the staging of two art exhibitions.

On returning to England, Prout continued to paint Australia subjects for a number of years. Between 1849 and 1853 he showed New South Wales and Tasmania landscapes at the annual exhibitions of the New Society of Painters in Water Colours. He also painted a diorama, shown in London in 1850, which was 'illustrative of convict and emigrant life'. Then in 1852, without actually returning to Australia to see the newly discovered goldfields, he and two English artists (who had never been to Australia at all) produced a panorama of 'A Voyage to Australia and a Visit to the Gold Fields'. Over twenty years later, sixty-three of his paintings were used as the basis of steel engravings in Edwin Carton Booth's *Australia Illustrated* (1873-76).

Both in Tasmania and in England Prout's finest works depicting Australian subjects were of tree ferns, especially in the 'Valley of Ferns' on Mount Wellington above Hobart. By the mid-1840s, when first visited by Prout, this fern tree gully had at least in part been ruined by picnic parties from Hobart. Nevertheless, in several of his paintings, Prout showed the gully as an unspoilt retreat for Aboriginals, who by then had been exiled to Flinders Island — an anachronism common to many artists when painting this type of subject.

Prout's celebration of the 'Valley of Ferns' in his paintings was part of the 'fern craze' which was at its height in both Australia and England in the mid-nineteenth century. To Prout, the fern tree was 'perhaps the most elegant production of nature' in Tasmania. To his English audience, the most remarkable aspect of these paintings was the difference in size between English ferns and Australian tree ferns. As the English journal, the *Athenaeum*, noted in discussing one of his paintings:

> In the *Valley of Ferns, Hobart Town*, the lowly plant of our hedges and banks is seen emulating in scale the stately tree. The other vegetation is equally gigantic.

John Skinner Prout
In the Valley of Ferns, Hobart Town, Tasmania
  c.1851
watercolour
39.0 × 60.0 cm
Art Gallery of New South Wales

William Duke

1815-1853

William Duke was one of a number of colonial artists who primarily worked as 'scenic artists', painting theatrical scenery, but who also executed a number of exhibition paintings. Most of these artists would probably have preferred to work exclusively as 'true' artists, but were unable to support themselves as such. For the same financial reasons, even a number of the more successful colonial artists occasionally turned to scene painting. Early in 1842 John Skinner Prout spent several weeks painting scenery for the Olympic Theatre in Sydney. In 1863 Nicholas Chevalier, the most successful Melbourne artist of the mid-1860s, painted the drop scene for Edgar Ray's diorama, *Christmas in England*.

Duke, who came out from Ireland to Australia in 1840, worked first in Sydney, then Auckland and Hobart and, finally, Melbourne, where he died in 1853. Throughout this period Duke worked as a scenic artist, but in Auckland he began painting portraits. In Hobart, where he lived from 1845 until about 1850 and painted most of his Australian pictures, Duke made something of a specialty of painting marine subjects. Because these pictures depict various aspects of the Tasmanian whaling industry, which was then at its peak, they are among the most interesting colonial marine paintings.

In most of his whaling pictures Duke either painted 'portraits' of the whaling ships or depicted the process of whaling. While his ship portraits were probably commissioned by either the owners or captains of the vessels, many of whom were very prosperous, Duke appears to have had difficulty selling his paintings showing the process of whaling, even though they could have appealed to a broader audience by not depicting specific ships. As noted by one Hobart newspaper when reviewing Duke's series of lithographs, 'The Chase', 'The Rounding', 'The Flurry' and 'The Cutting In', such subjects were 'interesting to all here', not only 'as displaying the scenes of unrivalled hardihood and courage in our whalers, but as being one from which we derive a very principal share of the resources of the colony'.

Outstanding among Duke's whaling pictures is *Offshore whaling with the 'Aladdin' and 'Jane'* which combines two ship portraits with a dramatic whaling scene. At left is the barque *Aladdin*, a British naval vessel which was converted into a whaler and which from 1847 worked out of Hobart for almost fifty years. In the centre of the picture is the *Jane*, which worked only briefly from Hobart in the mid-nineteenth century. In the foreground there is an extraordinary frenzy of activity with some of the whaleboats afloat, while others are sinking with their crews partly in the water.

William Duke
Offshore whaling with the 'Alladin' and 'Jane' 1849
oil on canvas
86.7 × 103.6 cm
Tasmanian Museum and Art Gallery

S.T. Gill
1818-1880

Shortly after arriving in Adelaide in 1839, S.T. Gill advertised that he had opened a studio where he sought:

> ... the attendance of such individuals as are desirous of obtaining correct likenesses of themselves, families, or friends ... Correct resemblances of horses, dogs, etc., with local scenery, etc., executed to order. Residences sketched and transferred to paper suited for home conveyance.

The substance of Gill's advertisement was his willingness to paint any type of commission, and over the following forty years he painted a greater range of subjects than any other colonial artist. Apart from portraits of the colonists, their animals and houses (as specified in his advertisement) and paintings of life on and around the Victorian goldfields, (for which he is best known), Gill painted street scenes and city views, landscapes and rural scenes, Aboriginal and exploration subjects and a range of topical events.

Gill, who had some training as an artist in Plymouth and London, worked in South Australia from 1839 until 1852. Although during this period he became Australia's first professional photographer and executed numerous lithographs, he was most important as a painter. Largely in response to commissions, he painted watercolours of the streets of Adelaide, its mansions, agricultural exhibitions and racehorses, as well as rural scenes, the copper mines at Kapunda and Burra, and the silver mines at Glen Osmond.

The most remarkable and romantic of Gill's South Australian paintings were the result of his one major sketching trip in the colony, his participation in 1846 as an unpaid member of an expedition into the interior led by John Horrocks. The object of this expedition was to discover new grazing land in the country about Lake Torrens, to the north of Spencer's Gulf. However, when the men reached the lake now known as Lake Dutton, to the west of Lake Torrens, Horrocks accidentally shot himself and subsequently died of

S.T. Gill
Invalid's tent, salt lake 75 miles north-west of mount Arden 1846
watercolour
21.4 × 34.2 cm
Art Gallery of South Australia

S.T. Gill
First Subscription Ball, Ballarat 1854
watercolour
25.1 × 35.3 cm
City of Ballarat Fine Art Gallery

S.T. Gill
The drawing room of Monsieur Noufflard's house
 1857
pencil and watercolour, heightened with Chinese white
16.7 × 23.7 cm
private collection

S.T. Gill
**The first cricket match between New South Wales
and Victoria, played in the Sydney Domain in
January 1857** 1857
watercolour
30.9 × 49.4 cm
National Library of Australia

gangrene. Only Gill, in any sense, profited from the expedition. In paintings such as *Invalid's tent*, which shows the artist waiting outside Horrocks' tent while another member of the party went for help, Gill was very successful in depicting both the course of the expedition and the desert scenery. Notwithstanding that paintings of this type were regarded as presenting scenery of the 'most inhospitable and desolate appearance' — demonstrating 'how very impossible it is that any stations can be made to the west of Lake Torrens' — Gill found a ready market for these works in Adelaide.

After losing the use of his right hand through inflammation and then declaring himself bankrupt during 1850-51, Gill set off for Victoria where he remained for four years. During this period, which he spent partly on the diggings at Mount Alexander, Bendigo and Ballarat, and partly in Melbourne, Gill's most important works were lithographs, especially those illustrating life on the goldfields. However, he also painted many watercolours of the diggings, including several paintings of life in the Red Hill area of Ballarat, where various concert halls, the circus, the Adelphi Theatre and the Assembly Rooms were located. In these paintings, such as *First Subscription*

Ball, which depicts the first of the series of grand balls held to mark the opening of the Assembly Rooms in October 1854, Gill vividly captured the diggers at play.

In 1856 Gill moved to Sydney, probably because he had saturated the market for his style of art in Victoria and had also encountered considerable competition from artists such as Eugene von Guérard and Nicholas Chevalier who settled in Melbourne in the mid-1850s. Especially during his first years in Sydney Gill was quite successful, executing numerous lithographs and painting many watercolours depicting a wide range of subjects. However, as a result of increasing alcoholism as well as venereal disease which he had contracted at the diggings, both Gill's output and the quality of his work steadily declined.

One of Gill's early works in Sydney was *The first cricket match between New South Wales and Victoria played in the Sydney Domain* (1857), which records what was, in fact, the second cricket match between the two colonies, though the first to be played in Sydney. The painting is one of at least three by Gill of intercolonial and international cricket matches which in the mid-nineteenth century engendered considerable public, and hence artistic, interest. Many of these games were the subject of prints and photographs as

S.T. Gill
Night 1870
watercolour
29.1 × 44.9 cm
Australian National Gallery

well as paintings. In the case of the New South Wales-Victoria match of 1857, both Gill and the Sydney artist Joseph Fowles produced lithographs of the game. In addition, a topical song with sheet music was published which had 'for a vignette a spirited sketch of the cricket ground in the Outer Domain, with cricketers at play'.

Gill's early Sydney paintings also included a commission to paint eight watercolours of a house in Bligh Street in the city, rented by a French wool merchant, Monsieur Noufflard. Many wealthy colonists commissioned colonial artists to paint views of the exteriors of houses, sometimes even from two or more aspects. However, Noufflard not only commissioned views of his house as seen from the street, its verandah and courtyard. He also commissioned Gill to paint his drawing room and office, and even his kitchen and bedroom. The resultant paintings, which show an unpretentious middle-class establishment, are the earliest known set of pictures which depict both the exterior and interior of an Australian home.

In 1862 Gill returned to Melbourne where, until his death in 1880, he used his declining skills to rework the subjects of his earlier watercolours and prints. As a result, contemporary city life became much less

important in his work. Instead, in paintings such as *Night* (1870), which treats a subject he had first attempted at least fifteen years previously, Gill focused on pastoral life and the goldfields, recalling the defeats and triumphs, hardships and pleasures of the stockmen, shepherds and diggers of the 1850s.

John Michael Crossland

1800-1858

For a brief period, from the late 1840s until the early 1850s, Adelaide became the most important centre of colonial art. Attracted by South Australia's strong economy and the enthusiasm for the fine arts of several of the colony's leading citizens, there was a considerable influx of artists. In addition to a number of artists who moved to Adelaide from other colonial capitals, several came from Europe, including John Michael Crossland and Alexander Schramm.

Crossland, who studied at the Royal Academy schools in London, exhibited occasional portraits and subject pictures at the Royal Academy and Royal Society of British Artists between 1832 and 1844. In 1851 he emigrated to Adelaide and, until his death seven years later, was the colony's finest portrait painter, executing portraits of many prominent South Australian colonists including the Governor, Sir Henry Young, the Chief Justice, Sir Charles Cooper and the explorer, Captain Charles Sturt.

Exceptional in Crossland's oeuvre are two portraits, painted in 1854, of Aboriginals who were then resident at the Poonindie Mission station just north of Port Lincoln in South Australia. The Poonindie Mission had been established in 1850 by Archdeacon, later Bishop, Mathew Blagden Hale, as a 'Christian village of South Australian natives, reclaimed from barbarism and trained to the duties of social Christian life'. Initially the mission served only as an advanced training centre for Aboriginals who had received their primary education at the Adelaide School for Aborigines. However, from 1853 it expanded to become a receiving centre for 'any persons of whatever age or sex, and whether half casts or wholly of the aboriginal race, as shall be sent ... by the Protector of Aborigines'.

Hale commissioned Crossland's paintings as records of his achievements at Poonindie. It seems he not only selected appropriate Aboriginals and sent them to Adelaide to sit for their portraits, but also determined the roles in which they should be presented. One of the portraits is of Samuel Conwillan, the outstanding 'success' of Poonindie in the 1850s, who was 'as adept at driving a bullock as he was at taking a church service' and was depicted by Crossland, Bible in hand as if ready to take a service. In the other portrait of the boy Nannultera, Crossland recorded another 'proof' of the Aboriginals' 'progress at civilization' at Poonindie — the successful introduction of cricket.

As Crossland's portraits indicate, the Poonindie Mission was in its own terms very much a success. According to a visitor to Poonindie in 1853:

At half past six in the morning and in the evening after sundown all assemble at the Archdeacon's cottage for the reading of Scripture and prayer ... After breakfast they go to their several employments: the cowherds milk... some were engaged in putting up posts and rails for a stockyard; the shepherds were with their flocks, two assisted the bricklayer... At the proper season they plow [sic], reap, shear, make bricks, burn charcoal, cut wood; do, in fact, under the direction of the overseer, the usual work of a station.

However, the portraits belie the fact that throughout the 1850s the Aboriginals at Poonindie suffered an extraordinarily high mortality rate as a result of being confined to tiny, unhygienic quarters to which they were not accustomed. Nothing is known of what happened to Nannultera, but Conwillan died in 1860, probably of some kind of lung disease.

John Michael Crossland
Nannultera, a young Poonindie cricketer 1854
oil on canvas
99.0 × 78.8 cm
Rex Nan Kivell Collection, National Library of Australia

Alexander Schramm

1814-1864

Alexander Schramm was the leading painter of figure subjects in Adelaide in the mid-nineteenth century. Born in Berlin, Schramm exhibited portraits and genre paintings at the Berlin Academy between 1834 and 1838, when he went to Warsaw, and again from 1844 to 1848, on his return. In 1849 he emigrated to South Australia where he painted several portraits of his fellow colonists, as well as numerous pictures of the local Aboriginals who form the subject of most of his extant work.

At least in their oil paintings (though not always in their prints and drawings) colonial artists generally ignored the destructive impact of European settlement on the Australian Aboriginals. Instead, Augustus Earle showed Bungaree as governor; John Glover attempted to suggest the 'happy' life of the 'pre-contact' Aboriginals; Thomas Bock was commissioned to depict noble savages who doubled as assistants to the settlers; Benjamin Duterrau celebrated the peaceful resolution of conflict between the Aboriginals and the colonists; and John Crossland was commissioned to portray 'civilised' Aboriginals.

Compared to these artists, Schramm found little to celebrate in the lives of the Aboriginals. Although he did not record the devastating impact of European settlement on the Aboriginal people of the Adelaide Plains, he did at least indicate that they benefited little from white society. Dressed in cast-off European clothes or draped in blankets, Schramm's Aboriginals play cards, barter with the Europeans or, as in *An aboriginal encampment*, simply congregate around their wurlies and fires.

Perhaps surprisingly, given his choice of subject, Schramm received some recognition and found a considerable market for his paintings of Aboriginals. At the 1861 exhibition of the South Australian Society of Arts, his painting *Whites and Blacks* was awarded a ten-guinea prize 'for the best picture or drawing of any description, subject being Australian'. Shortly after his death in 1864, the *South Australian Register* noted that Schramm

> . . . was particularly happy in his groups of natives, corroborees, and other subjects in which the scenes and actions represented were essentially South Australian. Several wealthy colonists have purchased and sent home pictures by Schramm, whilst others are, and we hope will be, retained in the colony.

Alexander Schramm
**An aboriginal encampment, near the Adelaide
    foothills** 1854
oil on canvas
89.0 × 132.0 cm
Art Gallery of South Australia

Charles Hill

1824-1916

Charles Hill was one of a small group of colonial painters who were more important as promoters of art in Australia than they were as artists. Born in Coventry, England, and trained as a line engraver, Hill arrived in Adelaide in 1854 where he abandoned engraving and took up teaching. In addition to holding his own art classes, he worked as an art master at a variety of Adelaide schools. In 1856 he took a leading role in the establishment of the South Australian Society of Arts of which he was first president. Five years later he became master of the School of Design set up by the society.

While in South Australia, Hill manifested a clear interest in painting important events in the history of the colony. Apart from two figure paintings of history subjects, he executed a marine picture depicting the steamer *Admella* which foundered on a reef off Cape Northumberland on 6 August 1859 while sailing between Port Adelaide and Melbourne. The ship broke almost immediately into three, with the midships section disintegrating, while the forepart and poop were left with their decks out of the water. On the following day, two members of the crew managed to make their way to the shore. Tragically it was not until a week after the accident that boats managed to get to the *Admella* and rescue the twenty-two survivors of the 113 people who had set out from Adelaide.

During the week when rescuers sought to reach the survivors on the stranded vessel, the *Admella* cast a pall over life in Adelaide and Melbourne. Special editions of daily newspapers were published to satisfy the demand for news and, in the aftermath of the rescue, one book and two pamphlets were quickly published describing the events surrounding the wreck. A number of poets, including Adam Lindsay Gordon, wrote verses about the *Admella*. As with the wreck of the *Dunbar* near the entrance to Port Jackson in 1857, in which 121 people died, the wreck of the *Admella* also attracted considerable artistic interest. Apart from Hill's painting of 1860, both the Adelaide artist James Shaw and the Melbourne artist Frederick Woodhouse painted the *Admella*, while the Adelaide printmaker Heinrich Berger executed a lithograph of the wreck.

Hill's painting, *The Admella rescue*, does not show any of the survivors actually being taken off the wreck. Instead it depicts the *Admella* just before the survivors were rescued by one boat from the shore and a whaleboat and lifeboat brought from Portland. This triumph of the rescuers, after a succession of unsuccessful attempts to reach the *Admella*, was described by the artist, George French Angas, in his poem, 'The Wreck of the Admella':

'Ho! to the rescue now!'
Success to that brave band,
With willing heart and honest brow,
With sunburnt face, and roughen'd hand —
The sterling heroes of the land —
Who come, with glorious purpose high,
Resolved to do or die.
    The mountain waves they breast,
With eager oar and straining eyes;
Now, high upon the billows' crest,
The gallant life-boat seems to rest —
Now through the surf she flies;
Till, with one wild, exulting bound,
She gains her living prize.
    'They're saved!' let one triumphant shout
O'er all Australia's land ring out —
Their battle with the sea is done,
The final conquest nobly won!

Charles Hill
The Admella rescue 1860
oil on canvas
55.9 × 99.1 cm
Art Gallery of South Australia

Harden S. Melville

working 1837-1879

The long wave of emigration from Britain in the nineteenth century, which was at its height in the 1850s, provided artists with a variety of popular themes for paintings and prints. Artists who remained in England were primarily interested in the theme of departure: the sad farewell. Artists who visited or worked in Australia preferred the theme of separation, which they frequently expressed by showing a pioneer settler in a bush hut reading mail from 'home', that is, from Britain.

One of the most famous images in this genre was based on a painting by Harden S. Melville, who first exhibited at the Royal Academy, London, in 1837. Between August 1842 and January 1846, Melville visited Australia as artist on two British naval ships, the *Fly* and *Bramble*, which carried out the first hydrographic survey of the coast of north-eastern Australia.

Following his return to England, Melville painted *The squatter's hut: news from home*, which appears to have been based on his experiences while travelling in New South Wales for six weeks early in 1844. As converted into a colour print by the English printmaker, George Baxter, this picture became one of the most popular works depicting the theme of separation.

Whereas most paintings of the 'letter from home' are characterised by dull browns and greys, emphasising the isolation and loneliness of the colonist, *The squatter's hut: news from home* is very brightly coloured and has unusually cheerful content. Instead of depicting a single (lonely) squatter, Melville showed three European men in the hut. An Aboriginal, who stands in the doorway, has just delivered the squatter's letter and in his right hand displays the coin he has received for his services.

Comparisons with contemporary prints, drawings and descriptive accounts indicate that Melville's painting gives a broadly accurate representation of a squatter's first home in the bush: Aboriginals are

Harden S. Melville
The squatter's hut: news from home 1850–51
oil on canvas
87.8 × 102.1 cm
Australian National Gallery

Harden S. Melville
The squatter's hut: news from home 1850–51 (detail)
oil on canvas
87.8 × 102.1 cm
Australian National Gallery

present in a number of mid-nineteenth century representations of squatters' and stockmen's huts; white cockatoos were popular pets with the squatters; and the absence of women is also consistent with contemporary accounts of bush life.

The painting departs from historical accuracy, however, in at least a few respects. Bush huts were generally fairly rude bark and slab constructions, but Melville exaggerated the rustic character of his hut by including a large tree trunk as a beam and converting the door into a gothic arch. The Aboriginal mailman was also a creation of Melville's imagination —

although the artist may have had some factual basis for his apparently exotic dress, which is similar to that of two Aboriginals in a sketch by Melville of a scene on the Swan River in Western Australia. As if to explain the appearance of the Aboriginals in *The squatter's hut: news from home*, Melville later wrote:

> The character of savages is generally so marked in their physiognomy, and the decorations they wear are usually so hideous, that it requires very little artistic skill to make a decided caricature (if not a more exact delineation), the resemblance of which to the original would be at once perceptible.

Thomas Baines

1820-1875

Thomas Baines, an English artist who had considerable experience working in South Africa, was one of a number of European artists who came out to Australia as members of exploring expeditions. Whereas most of these artists, including Harden S. Melville, went to Australia on maritime expeditions, Baines came out for an expedition exploring the inland. Organised by the British Government at the instigation of the Royal Geographical Society, London, the objects of the North Australian Expedition were to investigate the source of the Victoria River in northern Australia, to provide information about the country's north-west interior, and to determine whether there was an inland sea or large river in the heart of the continent.

In the course of the North Australian Expedition, Baines had only limited time to devote to art. As he wrote subsequently:

> My time, in common with that of other officers and even of the commander himself has unavoidably been so much occupied with hard manual labour such as taking care of horses, attending to stores, working in boats and on board ship that I had little time for sketchings, and was less fit for it than if I could have given more time to my artistic duties.

Nevertheless, during the expedition, which lasted from August 1855 to November 1856, Baines succeeded in making hundreds of pencil, watercolour and crayon sketches of the topography of the country, of natural history subjects and of significant events which occurred during the expedition. Following the conclusion of the expedition he worked up some of these sketches into forty oil paintings which he delivered to the Royal Geographical Society in November 1857, together with four albums of his sketches.

Baines worked in Africa from 1858 to 1865 and it was only during an interlude in England between 1865 and 1868 that he returned to painting Australian subjects. In 1866 and 1867 he gave lectures in a number of English cities, illustrating his speeches with his own hand-painted magic-lantern slides of Africa and Australia. Early in 1867 he was also approached, through intermediaries, by the English publisher, Virtue & Son, who wanted to publish a large, illustrated book on Australia. Virtue had obtained:

> . . . a number of sketches by Prout of views in Australia ... But he wants sketches of parts into which Prout has never been, such as Western and Northern Australia, and ... [Baines was] the *only* man for those, or of the interior.

As a result, in 1868 Baines painted a series of six Australian subjects for engraving by Virtue, five of which are set in the Northern Territory.

In *Watering party of the North Australian Expedition* Baines depicted an event which occurred just under a month after the expedition had left Moreton Bay (Brisbane) for the estuary of the Victoria River in two ships, the barque *Monarch* and the schooner *Tom Tough*. For nine days in early September 1855, the *Monarch* was grounded on a reef near Melville Island, north of what is now Darwin. During this period an attempt was made to dig a well on the shore of a neighbouring island (Quail Island) in order to bring water to the suffering animals on board the ship.

Baines' *Gouty stem tree, Adansonia gregorii, circumference 58 feet*, which probably depicts the largest baobab tree seen by the artist in Australia, is linked to the most significant discovery made during the expedition by the botanist, Ferdinand von Mueller. Von Mueller established that the gouty stem tree, like the baobab tree of tropical Africa, constitutes a species of *Adansonia*. In honour of the North Australian Expedition's leader, von Mueller named the new species *Adansonia gregorii*.

Thomas Baines
Gouty stem tree, Adansonia gregorii, 58 feet circumference, near a creek south-east of Stokes Range, Victoria River 1868.
oil on canvas
45.2 × 66.5 cm
Australian National Gallery

Thomas Baines
Watering party of the North Australian Expedition under a clump of pandanus at Quail Island, Paterson's Bay 1868
oil on canvas
45.7 × 66.5 cm
Australian National Gallery

Robert Dowling

1827-1886

Robert Dowling was the first important colonial artist to be trained in Australia. Born in England, Dowling came out to Tasmania with his parents when he was seven and became a saddler. However, in the 1840s he also took drawing lessons from a number of Launceston and Hobart artists who may have included Thomas Bock. On the strength of this training, Dowling embarked on a career as a professional artist in 1850.

During the first half of the 1850s, Dowling worked in Launceston and then Hobart as a portrait painter, and also held drawing classes. Most, if not all, of his paintings executed in this period were competent, though unexceptional, portraits of single-figures,

frequently members of his family or their friends and acquaintances.

Dowling's work changed significantly when, probably in 1855-56, he went to Victoria. He painted a number of portraits in Melbourne but worked primarily in the Western District where he gained numerous commissions because he was the first figure painter of any competence and had extensive contacts with the squatters through his brother Thomas and sister-in-law Maria, who held Jellalabad station near Darlington. He continued to paint single-figure portraits but also began a series of ambitious group portraits which are his most important paintings. Some of these are of the squatters and their families; others are of Aboriginals.

Robert Dowling
Mrs Adolphus Sceales with Black Jimmie on Merrang Station 1856
oil on canvas, mounted on plywood
76.0 × 101.5 cm
Australian National Gallery

Robert Dowling
**Mrs Adolphus Sceales with Black Jimmie on
  Merrang Station** 1856 (detail)
oil on canvas, mounted on plywood
76.0 × 101.5 cm
Australian National Gallery

While working in the Western District, Dowling completed a group portrait for Mrs Adolphus Sceales (née Jane Paton) of Merrang station near Warrnambool. This painting, a tribute to, Mrs Sceales' late husband, Adolphus, who had died in 1853, is one of a number of commemorative pictures in colonial art. It is, however, unusual in its content. Whereas such paintings are generally portraits of the deceased person, based on a sketch or photograph, Dowling's painting does not include Mr Sceales. Instead, at the

right of the painting, Mrs Sceales, dressed in the mourning black of the mid-nineteenth century, stands beside her thoroughbred bay prepared to mount. At left, an Aboriginal groom known as Jimmie holds a large chestnut gelding hunter for an absent male rider, the late Mr Sceales.

After leaving Victoria, Dowling continued to paint group portraits of Aboriginals. While in Launceston he painted a picture of Victorian Aboriginals from the Geelong-Portland Bay district and a group portrait of Tasmanian Aboriginals, based on a series of portraits of Robinson's 'domesticated' Aboriginals painted by Thomas Bock in the 1830s (see p. 22). Then, after

going to London in 1857, he executed a very large picture, *A group of natives of Tasmania* (1859), which he sent back to Launceston as a gift to the people of the city. In 1860 he painted a small version of this large work before abandoning Australian subjects (except for two years at the end of his life when he returned to Melbourne and obtained numerous portrait commissions).

Painted at a time when almost all the full-blood Tasmanian Aboriginals were dead — and only one of the subjects of his pictures, Truganini, was alive — Dowling's group portraits of the Tasmanians were intended as historical documents recording the

appearance of the 'dying' race. This aspect of Dowling's work was repeatedly noted by contemporary commentators who, for example, wrote that 'as an historical picture' the large version of *A group of natives of Tasmania* would be 'invaluable'. However, the faces in Dowling's painting are quite different in colour and lacking the clarity of Thomas Bock's portraits. Moreover, Dowling used European models for his figures with the result that the proportions of the bodies, and especially those of the legs, are European in character and do not conform with what is known about the morphology of the Tasmanians.

Robert Dowling
A group of natives of Tasmania 1860
oil on canvas
45.7 × 91.5 cm
Royal Anthropological Institute of Great Britain and
    Ireland (on loan to the Australian National Gallery)

William Strutt

1825-1915

William Strutt was one of the few artists in Australia in the mid-nineteenth century with extensive training in figure painting. Born into a family of artists, Strutt studied in Paris for six years between 1838 and 1844. During this period he gradually passed through the academic curriculum which taught him to execute large-scale figure compositions. The first step in this very slow process was for students to study figure drawing from engravings, then from plaster casts and finally from live models. Later, students received instruction in painting. Only then were they taught composition.

When Strutt came out to Victoria in 1850 — after struggling to make a living as an artist in both France and England — he was the first academy-trained artist to arrive in the colony. Quite legitimately, he advertised his competence 'to execute Portraits in a style hitherto unattempted in these colonies', and in his first five years in the colony he succeeded in obtaining a small number of portrait commissions. Most of these pictures were of single figures which he painted in quite accomplished fashion. However, he was also commissioned by Dr Arthur O'Mullane, a wealthy Melbourne doctor, to paint his wife Maria and their four children. This group portrait in some respects appears naive, with its stiff figures and sharply falling floor, but this quality only results from the ambitious nature of the picture and Strutt's attempt to show his virtuosity by adopting a difficult 'fish-eye' perspective.

In the hope of eventual patronage Strutt also made numerous preliminary drawings for large-scale subject pictures and history paintings — particularly of the disastrous bushfire in Gippsland on 'Black Thursday' in February 1851, a day when according to Strutt:

> The heat had become so terrific quite early in the day that one felt almost unable to move. At the breakfast table the butter in the butter dish was melted into oil, and bread when just cut turned to rusk. The meat on the table became nearly black as if burnt before the fire, a few minutes after being cut.

However, there was no demand in the colony for large figure paintings and so Strutt supported himself primarily by working as an illustrator and teacher. Apparently disillusioned with his career as an artist, he went to New Zealand early in 1855 to try his hand at farming.

In mid-1856 Strutt returned to Melbourne and resumed his career as an artist. He later wrote that he found it much more difficult 'to make a new start ... than on my first arrival, for there was competition and but a slender demand for art'. However, he appears to have become at least as successful as during his first residence in Melbourne, obtaining several portrait commissions. Strutt also painted a small number of figure compositions, for example, of native troopers. However, he again failed to obtain any commissions for major paintings of Australian history subjects.

One of Strutt's first paintings following his return to Melbourne was a portrait of John Pascoe Fawkner (1792-1869). The son of a successful emancipist, Fawkner played a leading role in the foundation of the European settlement at Port Phillip Bay in 1835, was an important Victorian businessman and, from the introduction of responsible government in 1851 until his death, was a member of the colony's Legislative Council. Fawkner was also Strutt's most important patron and appears to have been idolised by the artist who felt that Victoria did not 'fully appreciate how much she owes to the labours and patriotism' of the 'indomitable' Fawkner. Perhaps surprisingly then, Strutt's half-length portrait of Fawkner shows a rather wistful figure, which contemporary critics were unanimous in praising as a good likeness, though it made Fawkner 'too good looking'.

Five years later, Strutt painted a posthumous portrait of Robert O'Hara Burke (1821-1861), the leader of the Victorian Exploring Expedition which was organised by the Royal Society of Victoria with the object of making the first crossing of the Australian continent. In mid-1860 the departure of the explorers from Melbourne had attracted numerous artists, including Strutt, to whom Burke gave a brief sitting for a portrait sketch. However the deaths of Burke and his deputy William Wills in 1861, while returning from the Gulf of Carpentaria, created even more artistic interest, resulting in several paintings over the next few years.

Of these pictures commemorating the expedition, the finest is Strutt's portrait of Burke, commissioned by the Melbourne Club of which the explorer had been a member. As the art critic, James Smith, wrote in January 1862:

> As a likeness it is striking, and as a work of art it possesses unusual merit. It is a full-length figure, the explorer being represented with his arms folded, and in an attitude habitual to, and thoroughly characteristic of, the man. The features are not merely faithfully reproduced, but the artist has also succeeded in impressing upon them much of Burke's character. His fiery outlook is slightly dashed with melancholy, as though he were forecasting some peril, or speculating upon some possible disaster, and the whole countenance wears a thoughtful but determined expression. The accessories of the scene — the recumbent camel and pack saddle, the arid plains tufted with salt bush, and the pallid lustre of the

William Strutt
Maria Elizabeth O'Mullane and her children c. 1852
oil on canvas
67.8 × 90.2 cm
National Gallery of Victoria

William Strutt
John Pascoe Fawkner 1856
oil on canvas
61.5 × 52.0 cm
National Library of Australia

William Strutt
Robert O'Hara Burke 1862
oil on canvas
98.0 × 64.0 cm
private collection

William Strutt
Black Thursday, February 6th 1851 1864
oil on canvas
106.0 × 319.0 cm
La Trobe Collection, State Library of Victoria

cloudless sky — have been skilfully subordinated to the general effect. All the details are finished with a Flemish minuteness and care, and no attempt has been made to idealise the subject. Burke stands before the spectator just as he lived.

Following his return to England in 1862, Strutt worked primarily at religious, animal and genre subjects. However, he also began to paint the rather melancholy, large-scale Australian history subjects for which he had begun to make preliminary sketches in Victoria. During 1862-64 he painted his spectacular Australian disaster subject, *Black Thursday*, recording the bushfire of 1851. In 1886-87 he painted *Bushrangers, Victoria, Australia, 1852* which depicts an incident which had occurred in Strutt's second year in Australia when four bushrangers bailed up and robbed seventeen people on the St Kilda Road in Melbourne. In 1911, just four years before his death, he painted *The burial of Burke*.

In painting these works as speculations, Strutt had only mixed success. When he showed *Bushrangers* at the Royal Academy in London, in 1887, it was bought by Charles Brooke Crawshaw, a Yorkshire colliery owner. However, it took more than twenty years before Strutt sold *Black Thursday* though during this period two unsuccessful attempts were made to acquire the picture for an Australian public collection. The first attempt was by Victorian ex-colonists in London who sought to purchase the painting by subscription; then, in 1870, James Smith attempted to persuade the trustees of the Melbourne Public Library, Museum and National Gallery to acquire the picture. It was not until the early 1880s that the Adelaide dealer, E.J. Wivell, bought *Black Thursday* and, after touring the picture around Australia, ultimately sold it to a private collector.

Eugene von Guérard

1811-1901

Among the immigrants who came to Australia in the gold rush era of the 1850s, there were numerous artists who went to Victoria in the hope of making a lucky strike at the diggings. Generally these men searched for gold for a year or two. Then, prompted by lack of success, they reverted to their original profession, as artists, in Melbourne or one of the goldfields towns.

Of these artists, by far the finest was Eugene von Guérard, who was born in Vienna and studied in Rome and Dusseldorf. On his arrival in Australia in December 1852, von Guérard worked for over a year on the Ballarat goldfields before going to Melbourne where he set up as an artist. He briefly experimented with figure painting, but this was not his strength as an artist and there was also only limited demand for this kind of painting. As a result he concentrated on landscape painting, which had been his main pursuit in Europe and for which there was a considerable local market.

Almost every year from 1855 until 1864, von Guérard went on at least one, and sometimes as many as three, major sketching expeditions. Thereafter he travelled less frequently, especially following his appointment in 1870 as Master of the School of Art and Curator of the National Gallery of Victoria in Melbourne. On most of these trips von Guérard stayed in Victoria but he went twice to Tasmania and once to South Australia and New South Wales. On his Victorian trips von Guérard's primary purpose was to find suitable subjects and patrons for his oil paintings. However, he made his more distant expeditions out of a genuine desire to see Australia as well as to make sketches for an album of views of Australian scenery, his volume of lithographed *Australian Landscapes*, which was finally published in 1866-68.

On most of his trips within Victoria, von Guérard combined visits to homesteads with exploration of less settled regions. By doing so he was able to obtain commissions to paint 'homestead portraits' from the squatters who in the 1850s and early 1860s were perhaps the most important group of art patrons in Victoria. He was also able to make sketches of wilderness subjects such as waterfalls and mountains

Eugene von Guérard
From the verandah of Purrumbete 1858
oil on canvas
51.4 × 86.3 cm
Australian National Gallery

Eugene von Guérard
Woodlands 1869
oil on canvas
91.7 × 156.7 cm
Australian National Gallery

Eugene von Guérard
Woodlands 1869 (detail)
oil on canvas
91.7 × 156.7 cm
Australian National Gallery

Eugene von Guérard
Forest scene near Kiama 1863
oil on canvas
35.8 × 56.0 cm
Australian National Gallery

Eugene von Guérard
Forest scene near Kiama 1863 (detail)
oil on canvas
35.8 × 56.0 cm
Australian National Gallery

which he generally painted as speculations and offered for sale in his studio or at public exhibitions in Melbourne. Von Guérard almost certainly preferred these romantic subjects to homestead portraits. However, he earned insufficient income from his wilderness views to be able to decline homestead commissions from the squatters had he been so minded.

Von Guérard's earliest homestead portraits are of Purrumbete, a cattle station situated on Lake Purrumbete, ten kilometres east of Camperdown in the Western District of Victoria. Von Guérard visited Purrumbete in November 1857 and in the following year painted two reciprocal views of the station for its holders, John and Peter Manifold. *From the verandah of Purrumbete* looks east from the verandah of the house across the lake; *Purrumbete from across the lake* looks west across the lake towards the homestead. Whereas the latter of these paintings is a typical colonial homestead portrait in composition — presenting a straightforward view of the house — *From the verandah of Purrumbete* is exceptional for its compositional inventiveness. By taking the verandah as his vantage point, von Guérard transformed the rather featureless landscape into a strikingly interesting painting in which the rectangular

internal framing provided by the verandah posts, roof-beam and balustrade, set off by the graceful curves of the vines, becomes the dominant motif.

Eleven years later von Guérard painted his last and largest Victorian homestead portrait — a simple composition depicting Woodlands, a station on the headwaters of the Wimmera River, five kilometres north-west of Crowlands near Ararat. Von Guérard had visited Woodlands in 1864 but only received a commission from its owner John Wilson on a second visit in 1868. The reason was the conversion of the house in 1868 from a four-room cottage into a grand Italianate mansion, and the creation of a new garden which, apart from six or so large eucalypts, was turned over to a wide range of exotic trees and shrubs.

Consistent with the painting's role as a celebration of the building of the new mansion at Woodlands, the house is the focal point of the canvas. Yet, as in many of von Guérard's homestead portraits, the house is only a small object within the middleground. The bulk of the painting shows Woodland's rich pastures which provided the station's wealth and made John Wilson one of Victoria's 'shepherd kings'. In the foreground are two horsemen and a horsewoman who, in a general way, may be taken to represent the owners of

the station but do not represent specific individuals.

The people who commissioned von Guérard to paint homestead portraits were, of necessity, successful landholders, usually with substantial if not grand houses. The owners of small houses and bush huts typically could not afford to buy oil paintings. Nevertheless, such houses, especially when set against a background of virgin forest or dramatic mountains were a popular subject with many colonial artists because they could be used to convey the idea of the pioneer in the wilderness, the taming of the land.

One of von Guérard's rare attempts at painting this type of subject is *Forest scene near Kiama*, a product of his visit to New South Wales in 1859, albeit painted four years later with the aid of a detailed sketch. The picture depicts the pioneer theme by showing a primitive cottage set in a small clearing with a wall of forest behind. At the same time it celebrates the luxuriant rainforest vegetation which attracted numerous colonial artists, including von Guérard, to the Illawarra region in the nineteenth century.

When working without commissions, von Guérard generally chose to paint areas which had not yet been marked by European settlement. His preferred subjects were fern tree gullies, waterfalls, rocky coastal scenes and views of spectacular mountains as well as sweeping views from mountain tops. In these pictures von Guérard was concerned to convey the grandeur of Australian scenery. He probably also sought to convey the magnificence of God's creation; as he put it, 'to catch now and then a glimpse of the divine poetical feelings' inspired by nature. But most of all von Guérard 'wished to paint so closely as he saw the details and effects of nature'. As he stated:

> If ever ... [he] could succeed to paint Australian scenes to make them delightful illustrations for treatises of botanical or geological features of the colony then he would be convinced that for the future his paintings would have a greater value, where it will be doubtful if those which can be taken equally well for a misty English or an Australian landscape will have the same future.

Von Guérard's *Ferntree Gully in the Dandenong Ranges* depicts a site about forty kilometres east of Melbourne which in the late 1850s and in the 1860s was renowned for its beauty. Von Guérard made at least two sketching trips to the gully between 1855 and 1857 before painting his landscape which, as described by a contemporary critic, 'is equally valuable as a botanical study, as a depiction of one of the most characteristic features of Australian scenery'. In the foreground is a giant fern, identifiable as the soft tree fern *Dicksonia antarctica*. Manna gums also flourish in the gully, although the conspicuous dead

tree near the centre of the painting is more likely to be the mountain grey gum which covers the hill slopes. The large arching tree framing the composition from the left is not readily identifiable, but is probably the austral mulberry, *Hedycarya angustifolia*, common in this kind of gully but rarely so large.

Ferntree Gully in the Dandenong Ranges was by far the most famous Victorian painting of its day. It was the subject of unanimous contemporary acclaim and two unsuccessful public subscriptions, the first of which sought to acquire the painting for presentation to the Queen and the second of which sought to keep the painting in Australia 'as the beginning of a National Gallery'. Ultimately, in about 1859, the painting was sold privately to von Guérard's most important single patron, Frederick Dalgety, the merchant, financier and founder of the pastoral company, Dalgety and Company. Dalgety lived in England after 1859 and in 1862 he showed *Ferntree Gully in the Dandenong Ranges* to considerable praise at the London International Exhibition.

Von Guérard's painting of Steavenson Falls, situated about eight kilometres from Marysville in the Great Dividing Range in Victoria, conveys a similar image of nature. The Steavenson Falls, then known as the Bonyarambite Falls, are the highest in Victoria, dropping about ninety metres in three cascades. Von Guérard, who visited the falls in January 1862 and painted them the following year, did not, however, choose to dramatise the cascades. Instead, just as *Ferntree Gully in the Dandenong Ranges* shows a verdant, natural 'cloister' uninvaded by man, so his painting of Steavenson Falls shows a luxuriant, enclosed gully springing with life: Christmas bushes flower, ferns flourish, a kangaroo is surprised by the flight of a parrot.

Von Guérard's *North-east view from the northern top of Mount Kosciusko* shows a very different aspect of nature, celebrating the sublime or awe-inspiring elements of Australian scenery. As noted by one contemporary commentator:

> ... the chaos of old rocks, with ice and snow-covered slopes and peaks, and dark shadowy chasms reaching far down below the piled up columns of nature's masonry, are produced with wonderful effect. This picture alone is a complete rebuttal of the theory, if such a theory be now held by anyone, that Australian scenery possesses no elements of the sublime.

But the sublime did not appeal to all. Another critic wrote:

> Here we are high up among the clouds; rocks, rocks, rocks, on every side, huge shattered basaltic fragments; a deep crater-formed abyss at our feet, riven by subterrranean fires; the whole under a cold mantle of snow lying in the wildest confusion, flung

Eugene von Guérard
Ferntree Gully in the Dandenong Ranges 1857
oil on canvas
92.0 × 138.0 cm
Australian National Gallery

deep and thick in parts, with the black traprock showing through. Terribly true to nature, but most uncomfortable to look at.

Von Guérard visited the Mount Kosciusko region in November 1862 as one of a party led by the German scientist, Georg Neumayer, who was conducting a survey of Victoria — and at this point New South Wales — investigating terrestial magnetism. On 19 November, von Guérard's fifty-first birthday, Neumayer's party climbed first the Ram's Head, then Mount Kosciusko itself and finally what is now known as Mount Townsend, a peak a little to the north of Mount Kosciusko.

Von Guérard's *North-east view from the northern top of Mount Kosciusko* depicts the view from Mount Townsend, the second highest point in Australia, looking towards Mount Jagungal which is the large snow-capped peak visible on the horizon. In the middleground and background of the painting, von Guérard recorded the view accurately. In the

foreground, however, he introduced a large mound of boulders underneath which Neumayer and his scientific assistant, Edward Brinckmann, are depicted taking barometric readings to ascertain the height of the mountain. Von Guérard introduced these boulders into his painting in order to emphasise the physical insignificance of the men in the mountain landscape, and also to provide a link between foreground and background, and foreground and sky.

To von Guérard, *North-east view from the northern top of Mount Kosciusko*, which he painted shortly after his return from Mount Kosciusko to Melbourne early in 1863, was probably a picture of considerable personal significance. He would have been aware that he was the first professional artist to visit the Kosciusko region; he had climbed the peaks on his birthday, and the day had been a very eventful one. While Neumayer's party was on Mount Townsend 'a terrific gale set in from the west and the whole top of the mount was

Eugene von Guérard
**North-east view from the northern top of Mount
    Kosciusko** 1863
oil on canvas
66.5 × 116.8 cm
Australian National Gallery

enveloped in dense clouds, the rain falling in torrents'.
In the thick fog, the other three members of the party
became separated from Neumayer and von Guérard.
One of the party's two guides suffered exposure and
'became quite stiff and unable to move'. Neumayer's
assistant, Edward Brinckmann, was lost from the party
for eighteen days.

Much of this is conveyed in *North-east view from
the northern top of Mount Kosciusko* which von
Guérard clearly regarded as a record of Neumayer's
party on Mount Townsend — showing the
approaching storm at left, all five members of
Neumayer's party before their separation, as well as
Neumayer's dog, Hector. Inspired by the coincidence
of climbing a mountain of national significance on a
day of personal importance, von Guérard executed
one of his finest pictures, combining sublime scenery,
topography and illustration of Neumayer's party into a
successful whole.

Eugene von Guérard
Bonyarambite Falls 1863
oil on canvas
66.2 × 56.0 cm
Australian National Gallery

Nicholas Chevalier

1828-1902

Another of the artists who came out to Victoria in the 1850s was Nicholas Chevalier. Born in St Petersburg, Russia, of a Swiss father and Russian mother, Chevalier studied art and architecture in Lausanne, Munich, London and Rome, before sailing for Melbourne. From his arrival late in 1854 until he left Australia in 1869, most of his paintings were landscapes, though he also painted some portraits. Chevalier is now regarded as a much weaker painter than Eugene von Guérard but for a period in the mid-1860s he equalled and then surpassed von Guérard in reputation.

During Chevalier's first six years in Australia, from 1855 until 1861, he worked as a cartoonist for the weekly journal, *Melbourne Punch*. During this period he did not travel extensively in Victoria and most of his paintings were of European subjects for which there was a considerable colonial market. Among the few Australian landscapes he painted were *Studley Park at sunrise* (1861) and *The Survey Paddock at sunset* (1861), a pair of views depicting two of Melbourne's most popular recreation grounds on the Yarra River.

In 1861 Chevalier quit his position with *Melbourne Punch*, and over the next two years he went on two long sketching trips in Victoria with the German scientist, Georg Neumayer. As a result of these expeditions, Chevalier painted a large number of Victorian landscapes, including homesteads and views of more spectacular scenery. With these changes in subject, his reputation grew. In 1864 his large oil painting of the Buffalo Ranges, which combines a tamed foreground with wilderness background, won the competitive exhibition of Australian paintings for the newly established National Gallery of Victoria.

While travelling with Neumayer, Chevalier visited Mount Arapiles in the Wimmera district of north-western Victoria in May 1862. Late the following year he completed *Mount Arapiles and the Mitre Rock* for Alexander Wilson, brother of John Wilson, who in 1869 acquired von Guérard's painting of Woodlands (see p. 73). Since Alexander Wilson's landholdings included Mount Arapiles from March 1860 until 1884, the painting is a celebration not only of spectacular scenery but also of private property.

As recognised by Chevalier's contemporaries, *Mount Arapiles and the Mitre Rock* was one of his finest, large exhibition paintings. Writing in the Melbourne *Argus*, James Smith observed that Chevalier had painted this landscape with:

. . . a closer attention to finish than the artist has hitherto bestowed upon his paintings, and the result is a work of considerable pretensions and high merit. The scene portrayed is Mount Arapiles, a laminated mass of rock rising abruptly, and almost perpendicularly from the plain, and presenting the appearance of a large and dilapidated fortress, literally furrowed with age, and tufted with verdure. A portion of this singular bluff is flushed with the warm light of the westering sun, and another portion is softly veiled by the shadow of a passing cloud, in the gloom of which the isolated Mitre rock puts on a robe of imperial purple, which hue is also reproduced, together with some of the brighter tints of the sky above, in a pool of water, lying in sullen repose at the foot of the Mitre. Altogether Mr Chevalier has been fortunate in the selection of a subject, and skilful in its treatment.

Nicholas Chevalier
Mount Arapiles and the Mitre Rock 1863
oil on canvas
77.5 × 120.6 cm
Australian National Gallery

Nicholas Chevalier
The Survey Paddock at sunset 1861
oil on canvas
89.4 × 120.0 cm
Australian National Gallery

George Rowe

1796-1864

George Rowe also came to Victoria in search of gold but then set up as a landscape painter, contributing to the particularly strong tradition of landscape painting in Victoria in the second half of the 1850s and first half of the 1860s. Rowe, however, was exceptional among these artists because he depicted the diggings in much of his Australian work. Other artists whose careers followed a similar pattern, such as Eugene von Guérard, rarely painted the goldfields.

Rowe, who was born at Exeter, was one of the most prolific topographical printmakers working in England between 1820 and 1850. First in Hastings and then in the spa town of Cheltenham, he achieved considerable success with his topographic views and his business as a general lithographic printer, producing maps, circulars, tickets and so on for a wide range of clients. By the late 1830s he had become one of the most prominent citizens of Cheltenham. Between 1845 and 1847 he was High Bailiff of the town, a position equivalent to a present-day mayor. However, a number of Rowe's business ventures failed in the early 1850s, most significantly his redevelopment of the oldest Cheltenham spa, the Royal Old Wells. As a result, he set off for the Victorian goldfields, aged fifty-eight, in the hope of recouping his losses so as to be able 'to do something more than crawl on the face of the earth'.

Rowe arrived at Port Phillip late in 1852 and went to the Castlemaine goldfields, but illness prevented him from working on the diggings. He therefore set himself up selling provisions to other diggers at

George Rowe
Ballarat c. 1861
watercolour
61.8 × 153.6 cm
Dixson Galleries, State Library of New South Wales

Castlemaine and then established a canvas Eating and Coffee House at Bendigo. This venture also failed, and as a last resort Rowe returned to working as an artist. As he explained in July 1853, in a letter to his wife who had remained in England: 'One day I had but 6s. 2d. left, so I turned to my own profession, painted a few pictures not dreaming that I should be at all successful, but I was and soon got a few pounds together'. The following month he wrote to his daughter, 'How curious it is that I should come out digging and return to my own employment, and be so successful too.'

For about four years, Rowe remained in Bendigo. Initially he continued to sell goods as well as painting small watercolours, signs and, occasionally, theatre scenery. In a letter written early in 1854 he informed his wife, 'I have done pretty well today — took about £4 and an order for 2 signs 20/- each which I must do tomorrow — so you see I am all sorts of trades.' Early in 1857 he embarked on an ambitious series of fifty larger watercolours of scenes on the Bendigo and Forest Creek diggings, which were displayed in

Bendigo, Castlemaine and Melbourne and sold by lottery.

After two further years in Australia, during which he travelled extensively in Victoria and also visited Sydney and Hobart, Rowe returned to England. There he executed a series of large watercolours of Victorian and Tasmanian subjects which combine some foreground interest with distant, panoramic views. In 1862 he showed eight of these paintings, including *Ballarat*, in the Mining, Quarrying and Metallurgy section of the London International Exhibition. Because of their 'faithful and beautiful delineations of the country, workings and other relations of the gold fields', these pictures won Rowe one of the 500 prize medals awarded at the exhibition.

Thomas Clark

c. 1814-1883

Thomas Clark came to Victoria in about 1852, having been a moderately successful painter and teacher in England in the 1840s. In Melbourne he painted occasional portraits and figure subjects but worked primarily as a landscape painter and teacher. Until 1857 his landscapes appear to have been restricted to subjects in the vicinity of the city, such as St Kilda and the Yarra River. However, Clark then undertook a number of extensive sketching trips to South Australia, New Zealand and Victoria's Western District, where he visited the Wannon Falls, located immediately south of the small township of Wannon on the main road from Hamilton to Coleraine.

The Wannon Falls are not particularly spectacular. As one contemporary commentator noted, they are merely

> . . . a very respectable cascade . . . A width of one hundred feet, at least, and a perpendicular descent of one hundred and sixty feet, is not despicable for a Waterfall.

However, they *are* the largest waterfall in the Western District of Victoria and, reflecting the general importance of Western District subjects in Victorian painting in the 1850s and 1860s, became one of the most popular landscape subjects in colonial art. They were painted by S.T. Gill, Eugene von Guérard, Nicholas Chevalier and Louis Buvelot, but for Clark the falls became a specialty, forming the subject of at least seven of his landscapes. Clark appears to have sold some of these paintings in Melbourne but at least a few, including the version now in the Australian National Gallery, were bought by local landholders who wanted a record of one of the attractions of their neighbourhood.

Thomas Clark
The Wannon Falls c. 1860
oil on canvas
71.0 × 91.8 cm
Australian National Gallery

Henry Gritten
1818-1873

When Henry Gritten came to Victoria in 1853, aged thirty-five, he was an experienced, if pedestrain, painter of scenic 'views'. In England he had regularly exhibited at London's Royal Academy between 1835 and 1849, as well as at the British Institution and the Society of British Artists. In New York, where he lived from 1849 until 1853, he had exhibited at the National Academy of Design.

In Australia Gritten continued 'view' painting with limited success, which explains his many changes of residence. In 1854 he visited the Bendigo goldfields, Sydney and possibly Hobart. From 1856 until at least 1858 he was resident in Hobart. By 1860 he had moved to Campbell Town in central Tasmania to work as a photographer. In 1862 he was living in Launceston. Finally in 1864 he returned to Melbourne where he remained until his death in 1873.

For all his changes of residence in Australia, Gritten rarely ventured far out of the major cities for subjects for his paintings. In Hobart he executed numerous paintings depicting the 'standard' view of the city as seen from across the Derwent River with Mount Wellington as a backdrop; a view also painted, for example, by Joseph Lycett, Knut Bull and Eugene von Guérard. In Melbourne Gritten most often painted views of the city as seen from the Botanical Gardens and the Yarra and its tributaries.

When Gritten painted more distant subjects, he tended to do so after sketches by other colonial artists. In the case of *Granite boulders at the Black Hills near Kyneton* (1867), a subject about 100 kilometres north-west of Melbourne, Gritten based his painting on a photograph taken by the Melbourne photographer Frederick Cornell for the Kyneton Shire Council for the Intercolonial Exhibition held in Melbourne in 1866-67. The picture is the earliest documented example of a painting by a colonial artist being done from a landscape photograph.

Henry Gritten
Granite boulders at the Black Hills near Kyneton
1867
oil on canvas
40.6 × 55.9 cm
Australian National Gallery

Henry Gritten
Hobart Town 1856
watercolour
74.6 × 103.0 cm
Tasmanian Museum and Art Gallery

William Dexter

1818-1860

William Dexter was another of the artists who came out to Australia in search of gold. Having worked in England as a painter of china and then as a watercolourist, Dexter emigrated in 1852 and tried his luck on the Bendigo goldfields. He then resumed his career as an artist, working with little success in Sydney, Gippsland and Melbourne until his death in 1860. To supplement his income, he briefly conducted a school of design in Sydney and worked at 'Heraldic and Decorative Painting'.

Exceptionally for a colonial artist, Dexter was also involved in Australian politics. At Bendigo he took part in the revolt over the high cost of the miner's licence. Three years later, in Gippsland, he stood for Parliament as the 'working-man's candidate' but was 'shamefully defeated' by 133 votes to nine.

While in Australia, Dexter occasionally painted landscapes and portraits, but primarily executed still lifes and animal pictures. While most of Dexter's still lifes are quite conventional renditions of dead birds, his animal pictures are of greater interest. He painted a number of pictures of Australian fauna (now unlocated), including a very large *Death of a kangaroo*, which measured 213.5 cm x 152.5 cm, and an *Opossum by moonlight* which, as parodied by *Melbourne Punch*, was a 'portrait of an opossum who had been canonised and for that reason has been depicted as being surrounded with a nimbus or aureole'. As well, he executed a number of very English pictures of miniature spaniels, including *Lady's pet* which probably depicts a spaniel, called Phocion, owned by Dexter's wife, Caroline, whose initials are on the riding veil. Despite the personal nature of the painting's subject, Dexter attempted to sell *Lady's pet* in Melbourne in 1857 but when unsuccessful appears to have given it to his wife, who retained it after she and Dexter separated in 1858.

William Dexter
Lady's pet 1855
oil on canvas over cardboard
60.8 × 84.4 cm
Art Gallery of South Australia

Henry Short

1807-1865

Henry Short was an English artist who came to Victoria in search of gold in 1852 but from at least 1854 worked as an artist in Melbourne. Until his death eleven years later, Short painted a small number of landscapes, figure subjects and portraits, but mainly worked at the 'buffet' category of still life in which lavish displays of flowers and fruit are combined with expensive, ornate tableware. For at least a number of these dining-room pictures, Short found patrons in professional Melbourne.

In terms of composition, Short's work falls directly into the tradition of seventeenth-century Dutch still life painting, but he introduced a colonial element into many of his still lifes by depicting Australian fruit and flowers. With their abundance of objects, the paintings may be interpreted as standard Victorian *horror vacui*. Yet, as indicated by the titles which Short gave his work, they are also an embodiment of mid-century optimism, representing the richness and abundance of the land. To one of his pictures, *Victorian happy home*, Short tacked Byron's line 'Fair Clime, where every season smiles'. To another painting, *Colonial fruits and flowers in January*, he attached Spencer's verse, 'There is continual harvest here'.

Short's most interesting painting is *In Memory of the Lamented Heroes of the Victorian Exploration, 1861*, a tribute to the Burke and Wills expedition. Set against a backdrop of eucalypts (rather than the conventional interior of still lifes), Short adapted his standard 'buffet' subject to history painting. On the commemorative cup in the centre of the picture, he painted the portraits, from left to right, of Wills, Burke and Gray who had all died while returning from the Gulf of Carpentaria after achieving the first crossing of the Australian continent. At right, he included a locket of John King, who survived the expedition.

Among the many Burke and Wills pictures painted in Melbourne in the 1860s, Short's work is distinctive in two respects. Whereas most of these paintings were figure compositions depicting various tragic moments in the expedition — such as *The death of Burke, King's farewell look* — only Short approached this subject through fruit and flowers, which almost certainly have symbolic significance in his painting. Short also had a personal connection with the Burke and Wills expedition. In June 1860 his son William, a minor landscape painter, had applied unsuccessfully to accompany the expedition as artist.

Henry Short
**In Memory of the Lamented Heroes of the Victorian
      Exploration 1861** 1861
oil on canvas
70.0 × 90.7 cm
La Trobe Collection, State Library of Victoria

Louis Buvelot

1814-1888

Louis Buvelot
Mount Fyans woolshed 1869
oil on canvas
58.6 × 93.8 cm
Australian National Gallery

In 1865 — roughly ten years after the arrival in Victoria of Eugene von Guérard, Nicholas Chevalier, Thomas Clark and Henry Gritten — a Swiss landscape painter, Louis Buvelot, arrived in Melbourne. Prior to his arrival in Australia, Buvelot had also worked as an artist in Brazil and India. In Melbourne he spent a year working as a portrait photographer, but he then reverted to working exclusively as a landscape painter. By about 1870 he had become established as Melbourne's leading artist, a status he retained until the early 1880s when he ceased painting due to ill-health.

Buvelot owed his success in Australia to a number of factors. He won considerable acclaim for the breadth of his technique (which offered a stark contrast to the great precision with which von Guérard

painted). As noted by the leading Melbourne art critic, James Smith, Buvelot's paintings were:

. . . executed with an apparent carelessness which a closer examination convinces you is the ease and freedom of a practised hand secure of its results and disdainful of tedious detail, since all the desired effects are capable of being produced by a few decisive touches.

Buvelot also won acclaim for his choice of subjects — his focus on apparently non-descript aspects of the settled countryside, generally close to Melbourne. He was applauded for his ability to 'produce a picture at once truthful and pleasing' with 'the simplest materials in the way of landscape — a few gum trees, a water hole, and a distant mountain-range'.

Both these aspects of Buvelot's art followed

Louis Buvelot
Near Fernshaw 1873
oil on canvas
69.0 × 122.2 cm
Australian National Gallery

changes in European art and taste. By the second half of the 1860s, the French Barbizon artists, who worked in a similar mode, had achieved renown, and their influence was felt across Europe as well as in many European colonies and ex-colonies. In England successful members of the Royal Academy, such as Frederick Lee and Thomas Creswick, were acclaimed for their ability to elevate the familiar and commonplace in the landscape to the dignity of art.

These changes in taste were transmitted to Victoria where they were adopted by a new class of patron. Whereas von Guérard, Chevalier and Clark had won considerable patronage from squatters, especially those in the Western District, Buvelot sold most of his paintings to Melbourne's growing middle class of merchants, civil servants and professional men.

The only squatters among Buvelot's important patrons were the Cumming brothers, John and William, for whom he painted his only known 'homestead portraits'. John Cumming's station was Terrinallum, to the north of Camperdown in the Western District of Victoria. William Cumming held the neighbouring property of Mount Fyans. When Buvelot visited the brothers' stations in 1868, John Cumming

was living at Terrinallum, but William had left Mount Fyans to the care of managers and was living in Melbourne.

After painting a very large view of Terrinallum in 1869, Buvelot executed a pair of moderate-sized paintings of Mount Fyans for William Cumming who wanted these pictures for his Melbourne home. In one painting, Buvelot showed the homestead; in the other, he depicted the station's woolshed and sheepwash, with Mount Elephant on the horizon at left and the Cloven Hills on the right. Two years later, John Cumming commissioned four small views of Terrinallum which he sent to his son John who was then studying law at Trinity Hall in Cambridge, England. The paintings were intended to remind the young Cumming of Australia, and a contemporary photograph shows the four pictures decorating his Cambridge room among rowing oars and similar trophies.

Equally uncharacteristic of Buvelot's work as homestead portraits are his pictures of fern vegetation. In the 1850s and 1860s, Melbourne artists led by von Guérard had generally chosen to paint low-lying fern gullies such as Ferntree Gully in the Dandenong

93

Louis Buvelot
View near Heidelberg 1866
oil on canvas
37.8 × 55.2 cm
Australian National Gallery

Ranges (see p. 77). But in the 1870s and 1880s, led by Buvelot, they began to paint the hillside fern vegetation around Fernshaw, which is situated near Healsville, about sixty-five kilometres north-east of Melbourne, close to the crest of the Great Dividing Range. Contemporary commentators appreciated Fernshaw both for the richness of its ferns and for its gum trees which, as shown in Buvelot's *New Fernshaw*, are not 'grotesque and tortuous' but 'straight and tapering as a ship's mast, with but few branches and little foliage'.

Although there was considerable tree-felling around Fernshaw in the 1870s, in his paintings of the region Buvelot depicted the forest in its virgin condition and ignored the effects of the timber-splitter's work. The small figure of the splitter and his horse in *New Fernshaw* appear as humanising rather than as destructive elements within the landscape. The stretch of corduroy road, where timber has been placed at the crossing of a stream in the foreground, gives evidence of the splitters' productive labour, and the negative implications of environmental destruction are not explored.

The bulk of Buvelot's Australian paintings depict the settled countryside — with winding country paths or dirt tracks, a passing timber-splitter or country woman, a few head of sheep or cattle, a stagnant pool or dry creek, a few large gum trees. Most of his subjects were close to Melbourne, around places such as Lilydale and Mount Macedon, which were popular with excursionists from Melbourne and hence were known to Buvelot's urban middle-class patrons. But many of his subjects were from more distant parts of Victoria, resulting from Buvelot's journeys through the colony which began with a sketching trip to the Western District in 1867. Even these subjects, however, generally had a commonplace, and hence familiar, aspect to Buvelot's audience, and it was this familiar quality of Buvelot's paintings that was at the heart of his success.

Among the earliest of these paintings of the settled countryside by Buvelot is *View near Heidelberg*, which he painted in 1866 when he was still working as a city photographer and his sketching trips were confined to the immediate vicinity of Melbourne. In this period, Buvelot was particularly attracted by the Yarra Valley farmlands, including the area around Heidelberg, which is only twelve kilometres from the centre of the

Louis Buvelot
Near Lilydale 1874
oil on canvas
46.0 × 69.0 cm
Australian National Gallery

city and in the mid-1860s was still very much a rural backwater.

Similar in subject is *Near Lilydale* (1874), which clearly reveals the great difference between Buvelot's paintings and those of the colonial artists who had preceded him. The main features of the landscape — sunlit gum-trees and background hills, and rough pastures with cattle at water in a shadowed foreground — are commonplace, and the unspecific nature of the scene is indicated by its title. The focus of the painting is not a great panorama spanning the background as in many of the landscapes painted by Conrad Martens, Eugene von Guérard and Nicholas Chevalier. Instead, the view is taken from a low vantage point, the landscape is enclosed, and the foreground holds the main interest.

William Ford

c.1820-c.1886

William Ford was one of a number of artists who achieved some popularity in Melbourne in the 1870s while working very much in Louis Buvelot's shadow. An English artist, Ford sent examples of his work to Melbourne in 1870 in order to establish his reputation before his arrival. He appears to have emigrated the following year and, until he went blind in 1883, painted many Australian and English landscapes, numerous flower pictures and a few portraits.

Like several of his contemporaries in Melbourne, Ford followed Buvelot in finding his landscape subjects either within the city or in the settled countryside in its immediate vicinity. However, Ford did not emulate Buvelot's relatively broad style of painting or his celebration of the commonplace. Moreover, in many of Ford's paintings, figures play an important role, verging on narrative.

In the mid-1870s Ford was one of several artists who painted Hanging Rock near Mount Macedon, which was itself one of the most popular Victorian painting grounds. In the 1850s Hanging Rock had attracted artist-scientists from Melbourne because of its unusual geological formations. Twenty years later it was painted by Ford and other Victorian landscape painters because it had become a major tourist attraction, which in turn created patronage for art depicting the area. As illustrated in Ford's painting, it was

> . . . resorted to by visitors in search of natural beauties and by picnic parties innumerable at holiday times. About Christmas and New Year the grass is trodden to the bare earth in all directions. People clamber up the hill in thousands and explore the labyrinths formed by the complication of rocks . . .

William Ford
At Hanging Rock 1875
oil on canvas
78.9 × 117.3 cm
National Gallery of Victoria

Emma Minnie Boyd

1858-1936

Emma Minnie Boyd (née à Beckett) was one of a number of women artists who increasingly contributed to the annual exhibitions of the Victorian Academy of Arts, first held in Melbourne in 1870. In the first exhibition, only three of the forty colonial artists were women; by 1875 nine of the fifty-three exhibitors were women; two years later sixteen of the eighty artists were women. Generally these women exhibited watercolours — the traditional medium of lady painters — but many of their works were oil paintings.

Boyd, the daughter of Sir William à Beckett, Chief Justice of Victoria, had her first art lessons at Madame Pfund's school in Melbourne. In 1875, at the age of sixteen, she began exhibiting with the Victorian Academy of Arts, and she subsequently showed her work at the Victorian Artists' Society and the Royal Academy, London. Though most of her early paintings were landscapes, she also exhibited a number of figure subjects. Initially her paintings were not for sale, but from 1877 she sought to sell her work.

Boyd's *Interior with figures, The Grange*, painted the year she began exhibiting with the Victorian Academy, is one of a number of pictures she executed of her home, The Grange, Harkaway, near Melbourne. However, the painting is not only a record of the interior of the Boyd family home, but also a genre painting in which the relationship between the young man and woman, dressed respectively in black and white, is echoed by that of the similarly coloured cats at left. While the young man gazes with admiration at his female companion who appears oblivious to his attentions, the roles of the cats are reversed: the female kitten, from her disadvantaged position on the ground, tries to attract the tom kitten on the chair which looks down on her, unmoved.

Emma Minnie Boyd
Interior with figures, The Grange 1875
watercolour
23.5 × 35.6 cm
Joseph Brown Collection

Louis Tannert
1834-c. 1909

Louis Tannert
The Eastern Market 1878
oil on canvas
71.0 × 81.5 cm
Australian National Gallery

Louis Tannert was one of the few colonial painters to specialise in genre subjects — scenes drawn from everyday life. Born in Dusseldorf, Tannert studied in Dresden and exhibited in Berlin and Dusseldorf in the 1870s before emigrating to Australia in 1876. For over three years he worked as an artist in Melbourne, and then moved to Adelaide where he was Master of the School of Painting at the National Gallery of South Australia from 1880 to 1893 and Curator at the Gallery from 1882 to 1889.

As recognised by contemporary critics, Tannert's paintings were a significant addition to Victorian art, since over the previous decade the English artist Chester Earles had been the only local artist to specialise in figure painting and most of his pictures were of religious and literary subjects. When Tannert first exhibited with the Victorian Academy of Arts in 1878, one Melbourne newspaper was glad to

. . . welcome, with satisfaction, the appearance in this exhibition of *genre* paintings of very great merit. Herr Tannert in this respect has supplied a long felt want . . .

Within this context, Tannert seems to have found a ready market for his paintings which generally depict

German scenes. He appears to have arrived in Melbourne with a number of such paintings and, because they sold quickly, continued to paint German subjects. His only known painting with an Australian subject is *The Eastern Market*, which depicts the market which stood at the corner of Bourke Street and Exhibition Street, Melbourne, until demolished to make way for the present Southern Cross Hotel.

Louis Tannert
The Eastern Market 1878 (detail)
oil on canvas
71.0 × 81.5 cm
Australian National Gallery

Frederick Woodhouse

1820-1909

Frederick Woodhouse senior was the most prolific animal painter to work in Australia in the nineteenth century. Born at Hadley just north of London in 1820, Woodhouse studied art first in Cambridge and then London, where he attended the Royal Academy and took lessons from the noted animal painter, John Frederick Herring, who strongly influenced his work.

In 1858 Woodhouse arrived in Victoria where he lived for the next fifty years. Although he sometimes attempted other subjects — especially landscapes — Woodhouse worked primarily as an 'animal artist' in Melbourne and Geelong. Especially among stock and station agents, masters of hunts, bookmakers and the owners and trainers of racehorses, there was strong demand for his work, with the result that Woodhouse became one of the most successful colonial artists.

During his long career, Woodhouse received several commissions to paint pet dogs, greyhounds and prize sheep and cattle but his principal subjects were horses. He painted some carriage horses and hunters but mainly depicted racehorses. Sometimes he produced 'group portraits' of a collection of horses either in the saddlery enclosure or on the racetrack, though generally his commissions were for single animals. These portraits tend to be straightforward documents, with the horse in the stable or on the racetrack with the jockey up. However, in painting Rajah, an Arab stallion at the New Hall Stud at Moonee Ponds, Woodhouse executed a more fanciful piece, embracing the convention probably developed by the eighteenth century English animal painter John Wootton, of portraying Arab horses in a simulated 'Arabian' setting in order to emphasise these horses' Eastern origin.

Frederick Woodhouse
Rajah, an Arab stallion, with his groom, Thombo
1876
oil on canvas
44.0 × 59.5 cm
private collection

Thomas Flintoff

c.1810-1891

Thomas Flintoff, like Henry Gritten, was an English artist who went first to America before coming out to Victoria in 1853 for gold. After a stint on the diggings, Flintoff settled in Ballarat in 1856 where he established a photographic gallery at which he worked both as a photographer and portrait painter. In 1872 he moved to Melbourne where he worked principally as a portrait painter but also executed some landscapes and animal pictures, and in 1889 briefly resumed his career as a photographer.

Flintoff's painting, *Henry F. Stone and his Durham ox*, is one of a number of colonial cattle portraits — paintings which tend to look like folk art as much because of the proportions of cattle when seen in profile as because of the competence of the artists. Most of these paintings were commissioned by the owners of the animals, such as Henry F. Stone, who had a long career in the meat trade, first as head shopman to a butcher in Melbourne and later as owner of dairy farms around Essendon and Footscray, where he established an abattoir. Occasionally these animal portraits were painted for other reasons, as in 1856 when the prizes awarded by the Port Phillip Farmers' Society 'included portraits of the stock exhibited, in lieu of medals, for those who preferred the former method of recording their successful competitions'.

Whereas it is rare for landowners to be depicted in 'house portraits', partly because of problems of scale, it was relatively easy to include the owners of animals in paintings of their stock, and colonists sometimes commissioned such paintings. Because of their combination of proprietor and animal, the role of these double portraits as documents of ownership is particularly manifest. This role is especially obvious in *Henry F. Stone and his Durham ox* in which Stone, a rotund man in overcoat and top hat, leaves no doubts as to his proprietorial role by pointing with his cane at his enormous animal.

Thomas Flintoff
Henry F. Stone and his Durham ox 1887
oil on canvas
82.5 × 122.9 cm
City of Ballarat Fine Art Gallery

H.J. Johnstone
1835-1907

Along with Thomas Flintoff, H.J. Johnstone was one of the many colonial artists who also worked as a photographer. As was the case with Johnstone and Flintoff, these men frequently aspired to work solely as artists, and sometimes achieved this aim.

Johnstone worked principally as a photographer until the early 1870s. In England he studied art at the Birmingham School of Design and then joined his father's photographic business. In Victoria, where he went in 1853, Johnstone tried his luck at the Bendigo diggings but then settled in Melbourne where he became senior partner in the photographic firm, Johnstone, O'Shannessy & Co.

During this period in Melbourne, Johnstone 'devoted every moment at his disposal to self-improvement and conscientious study' of art. He first attended life classes conducted by the sculptor Charles Summers and then obtained regular lessons from Louis Buvelot. In 1872 he began contributing to the annual exhibitions of paintings held by the Victorian Academy of Arts in Melbourne.

From the mid-1870s until the mid-1880s Johnstone was one of the most successful Australian landscape painters. He primarily painted Victorian scenery but around 1874 made at least one sketching trip to South Australia and thereafter found a substantial market for his paintings in Adelaide. Although Johnstone left Melbourne in 1876 for San Francisco, Paris and then London where he settled, he continued to paint Australian subjects which he sent back to Melbourne, Adelaide and Sydney with great success. In 1880 one of his landscapes became the first painting of an Australian subject to enter the collection of the Art Gallery of South Australia, and during 1883-84 two of his paintings were bought by the Art Gallery of New South Wales.

Buvelot was the landscape painter who had greatest influence on Johnstone's work. Although personal relations between the two artists were poor in the mid-1870s, from then until well into the 1880s Johnstone painted a series of landscapes in which he was heavily indebted to Buvelot's famous *Waterpool near Coleraine — sunset*. In these paintings, which include *Evening shadows* and are mostly scenes on or around the Goulburn River, Johnstone depicted very still stretches of water as seen around sunset, with one or two large gum trees the subject 'of a special and separate study' in the foreground.

At the same time Johnstone was considerably influenced in his painting by his experience as a photographer. The tonalities and finish of his work are in fact such that it has been suggested that Johnstone

H.J. Johnstone
Evening shadows 1882
oil on canvas
66.3 × 101.8 cm
Australian National Gallery

worked up many of his oil paintings from photographs. However, as noted by a contemporary critic, it may simply have been that when Johnstone 'began to work in oils his long practice in photographic colouring not unnaturally influenced him in aiming at a certain smoothness of surface and prettiness of style' reminiscent of photography.

106

W.C. Piguenit

1836-1914

Born in Hobart, Piguenit was the last major figure in the line of nineteenth century Australian painters of Romantic landscapes, which includes such artists as Conrad Martens, Eugene von Guérard and Nicholas Chevalier. Piguenit worked as a draughtsman in the Tasmanian Survey Office between 1850 and 1872, where he received some instruction in painting from one of his colleagues, Frank Dunnett. As early as the mid-1860s he exhibited paintings and executed his first lithographs, while in 1870 he showed photographs at the Intercolonial Exhibition held in Sydney. Two years later he resigned from the Survey Office, and soon set up as a professional artist. Over the following four decades, Piguenit painted many views of peaceful river and open pasture and highland subjects, and was sometimes considered to be most successful when treating these 'genial' subjects. However, he won greatest acclaim for his views of awe-inspiring nature.

Until 1880, Piguenit primarily painted Tasmanian wilderness subjects, based on sketches he made in the first half of the 1870s as an unpaid member of a series of exploring expeditions. These expeditions gave Piguenit exceptional knowledge of central and south-west Tasmania. As the *Launceston Examiner* stated in 1877:

> No other person, with the exception of that thorough bush traveller the late Mr. Scott ... knows more of Tasmania. He has traced the valleys of the rivers Derwent, Huon, Davey, Gordon and Pieman to their sources; has eaten his damper on the shores of lakes Pedder, Maria and St. Clair; has tunnelled through miles of horizontal scrub ... and has travelled on foot thousands of miles, frequently with knapsack of over 56lbs weight on his back.

In 1880, encouraged by Eccleston du Faur, de facto director of the Art Gallery of New South Wales, Piguenit moved to Sydney where he continued to paint Tasmanian subjects but also sought out spectacular scenery in New South Wales. One of his first sketching trips was along the Nepean River and, over the following decade, he painted several views of the Nepean Gorge. These pictures range from images of overpowering nature to more peaceful images such as *On the Nepean*, which combines quite imposing scenery, in the form of the cliffs, with the tranquility of the river. The beauty of this stretch of river was widely appreciated in the late nineteenth century. Writing in 1888, the Sydney critic, John Plummer stated:

> Claude never painted rocky gorges more romantic or more awe-inspiring than those which are to be found in many parts of Australia, and there are portions of the Nepean which, in their stately grandeur, rival, if not surpass the picturesque castellated heights that bound the lordly Rhine. We have, in fact, here in Australia all the essentials for the creation of a purely Australian school...

W.C. Piguenit
On the Nepean 1881
oil on canvas
106.5 × 92.0 cm
Australian National Gallery

Bibliography

My two main sources have been my two earlier books on Australian art, *Australian Colonial Paintings in the Australian National Gallery* (Canberra: Australian National Gallery/Oxford University Press, 1986) and *Images in Opposition: Australian Landscape Painting 1801-1890* (Melbourne: Oxford University Press, 1985). For additional biographical information on artists, I have drawn particularly on Joan Kerr (ed.), *Dictionary of Australian Artists. Working Paper 1: Painters, Photographers and Engravers 1770-1870, A-H* (Sydney: Power Institute of Fine Arts, 1984). Further biographical information on patrons and sitters for portraits comes from the *Australian Dictionary of Biography* (Melbourne: Melbourne University Press, 1966-81), 8 vols.

Additional references are:

INTRODUCTION: The reappraisal of the range of colonial painting was largely initiated by Daniel Thomas' *Australian Art in the 1870s* (Sydney: Art Gallery of New South Wales, 1976). Paintings of Aboriginals have been examined by Geoffrey Dutton, *White on Black: The Australian Aborigine Portrayed in Art* (Melbourne: Macmillan, 1974); house portraits by Howard Tanner, *Converting the Wilderness: the Art of Landscape Gardening in Colonial Australia* (Sydney: Australian Gallery Directors Council, 1979); George Tibbits, *William Tibbits 1837-1906: Cottage, House and Garden Artist* (Melbourne: Department of Architecture and Building, University of Melbourne, 1984); and *Portraits in the Landscape: the House Paintings of William Tibbits 1870-1906* (Sydney: Historic Houses Trust of New South Wales, 1984); animal portraits by Colin Laverty, *Pastures and Pastimes: an Exhibition of Australian Racing, Sporting and Animal Pictures of the 19th Century* (Melbourne: Victorian Ministry for the Arts, 1983). Important on still life is Garry Darby, *William Buelow Gould* (Burnie: Australian Gallery Directors Council, 1980); on marine painting, Caroline Wesley, 'William Duke', *Art Bulletin of Tasmania*, 1983, 24-35; on history painting, Tim Bonyhady, 'Benjamin Duterrau's Paintings of the Conciliation of the Tasmanian Aborigines', *Bowyang*, 3, 93-105; and Heather Curnow, *William Strutt* (Sydney: Australian Gallery Directors Council, 1980).

The review of the 1847 Sydney exhibition is in *Heads of the People: an Illustrated Journal of Literature, Whims and Oddities*, 28 August 1847, 145. For information on prices charged for portraits in the 1850s, see John Tregenza, 'Two Notable Portraits of South Australian Aborigines', *Journal of The Historical Society of South Australia*, 12, 23; James Smith's comments on history painting are in the *Examiner and Melbourne Weekly News*, 19 October 1861, 12-13. On Robinson as a booby, see C.M.H. Clark, *A History of Australia: II New South Wales and Van Diemen's Land 1822-1838* (Melbourne: Melbourne University Press, 1968), 137. For Claxton in India, see Kerr, *Dictionary*, 156.

Mary Morton ALLPORT: Geoffrey Stilwell, *Mary Morton Allport: A Commemorative Exhibition, 1831-1981* (Hobart: Allport Library and Museum of Fine Arts, 1981); Joan Kerr, 'Mary Morton Allport and the Status of the Colonial "Lady Painter"', *Tasmanian Historical Research Association*, 31, 3-17.

Thomas BAINES: The letter quoted, concerning *Australia Illustrated*, is William Howitt to Baines, 30 April 1867, MS 95, ANL.

Thomas BOCK: N.J.B. Plomley, 'Thomas Bock's Portraits of the Tasmanian Aborigines', *Records of the Queen Victoria Museum*, n.s.

18; N.J.B. Plomley, 'In Black and White: Some Biographical Notes on Thomas Bock, late of Hobart, Artist', *Tasmanian Historical Research Association*, 18, 149-56.

Emma Minnie BOYD: Patricia Anne Dobrez, 'Martin Boyd, the aesthetic temperament: a critical study', 1980, 18-20.

John CROSSLAND: John Tregenza, 'Two Notable Portraits of South Australian Aborigines', *Journal of the Historical Society of South Australia*, 12, 22-31. On Poonindie, see also, A. de Q. Robin, 'Mathew Blagden Hale and the Poonindie Experiment', *University Studies in History*, 5, 34-50.

William DEXTER: Michael Watson, 'William Dexter, 1817-1860: Some New Sources For His Paintings', *La Trobe Library Journal*, 9, 11-14. Dexter's election results are reported in the *Age*, 19 November 1857, 5.

Robert DOWLING: N.J.B. Plomley, 'Pictures of Tasmanian Aborigines', *Annual Bulletin of the National Gallery of Victoria*, 3, 17-22. The large version of *A group of natives of Tasmania* was discussed in the *Cornwall Chronicle*, 14 April 1860.

William DUKE: Caroline Wesley, 'William Duke', *Art Bulletin of Tasmania*, 1983, 24-35; Clifford Craig, *More Old Tasmanian Prints: a Companion Volume to the Engravers of Van Diemen's Land and Old Tasmanian Prints* (Launceston: Foot & Playstead, 1984), 308-9, 321-3.

Augustus EARLE: Harold Spencer, 'The Brisbane Portraits', *Journal of the Royal Australian Historical Society*, 52, 1-8; Eve Buscombe, 'A Discussion about Augustus Earle and Some of His Portraits', *Art Bulletin of Victoria*, 19, 46-59.

Thomas FLINTOFF: The animal portraits awarded as prizes by the Port Phillip Farmers' Society are noted in the *Argus*, 4 February 1856, 5. They were painted by S. S. Knights. Biographical information on Henry F. Stone comes from Lauraine Diggins Gallery, *Australian Colonial Fine Arts* (Melbourne: 1986), 11.

S.T. GILL: Shar Jones, *Monsieur Noufflard's House: Watercolours by S.T. Gill, 1857* (Sydney: Historic Houses Trust of New South Wales, 1984); Ron Appleyard, Barbara Fargher, Ron Radford, *S.T. Gill: The South Australian Years 1839-1852* (Adelaide: Art Gallery of South Australia, 1986). On the Red Hill area of Ballarat and the Assembly Rooms, see Weston Bate, *Lucky City: The First Generation at Ballarat 1851-1901* (Melbourne: Melbourne University Press, 1978). The *Cricket Match Schottische* is described in the *Sydney Morning Herald*, 17 January 1857, 10.

Charles HILL: R.G. Appleyard, 'Charles Hill (1824-1916)', *Bulletin of the National Gallery of South Australia*, 28, n.p. The most detailed account of the *Admella* is Ian Mudie, *Wreck of the Admella* (Adelaide: Rigby, 1966). George French Angas' poem was published in *The Wreck of the Admella and Other Poems* (Adelaide, 1874).

H.J. JOHNSTONE: The main biography is in the *Age*, 7 November 1891, 14. The relationship between Johnstone's photography and his painting is discussed in Ron Appleyard, Barbara Fargher, Ron Radford, *S.T. Gill: The South Australian Years 1839-1852* (Adelaide: Art Gallery of South Australia, 1986), 9; *Argus*, 27 April 1878, 9.

John LEWIN: Phyllis Mander Jones, 'John William Lewin: a Memoir', *Royal Australian Historical Society Journal and Proceedings*, 42, 153-86. Rex and Thea Rienits, *Early Artists of Australia* (Sydney: Angus & Robertson, 1963), 124-45.

Conrad MARTENS: Martin Terry, 'Conrad Martens and the Zig Zag', *Art and Australia*, 21, 503-6. The quotation discussing Martens soon after his arrival is from the *Australian*, 4 August 1835, 3.

John Skinner PROUT: A.V. Brown, 'John Skinner Prout — his Tasmanian sojourn 1844-48', *Art Bulletin of Tasmania*, 1984, 20-31; Tony Brown, 'John Skinner Prout — a colonial artist', *Art and Australia*, 22, 516-22. Prout discusses tree ferns in *Prout's Dioramic Views of Australia, Illustrative of Convict and Emigrant Life* (London: 1850), 9. The review of *The Valley of Ferns* is in the *Athenaeum*, 26 April 1849, 440.

George ROWE: Patricia Reynolds, 'George Rowe on the Bendigo Diggings', *La Trobe Library Journal*, 3, 90-95; Steven Blake, *George Rowe, Artist and Lithographer 1796-1864* (Cheltenham: Cheltenham Art Gallery and Museum, 1982).

Alexander SCHRAMM: R.G. Appleyard, 'Alexander Schramm, Painter', *Bulletin of the Art Gallery of South Australia*, 37, 26-41.

Henry SHORT: Jennifer Phipps, *Artists' Gardens: Flowers and Gardens in Australian Art 1780s-1980s* (Sydney: Bay Books, 1986), 48. See also William H. Gerdts, *Painters of the Humble Truth: Masterpieces of the American Still Life 1801-1939* (Columbia: University of Missouri Press, 1981), 87, for the work of Severin Roesen whose paintings provide an American parallel to Short's abundant still lifes.

William STRUTT: George Mackaness (ed.), *The Australian Journal of William Strutt, ARA 1850-1862* (Sydney, 1958); Heather Curnow, *William Strutt*, (Sydney: Australian Gallery Directors Council/Art Gallery of New South Wales, 1980). The portrait of the O'Mullane family has not previously been attributed but, as discovered by Roger Butler, is signed by Strutt within the carpet in the lower centre of the painting. The painting is discussed in Jennifer Phipps, 'Portrait of Maria Elizabeth O'Mullane and her children c. 1852', *Art Bulletin of Victoria*, 18, 53-5. Strutt's 1856 portrait of Fawkner was reviewed in the *Argus*, 27 October 1856, 6; 18 December 1856, 7; *Age*, 15 December 1856, 5; 20 December 1856, 4. His portrait of Burke was reviewed in the *Argus*, 29 January 1862, 5.

Louis TANNERT: *Illustrated Australian News*, September 1877, 5, 10; *Daily Telegraph*, 27 April 1878, 5.

Thomas Griffiths WAINEWRIGHT: Robert Crossland, *Wainewright in Tasmania* (Melbourne: Oxford University Press, 1954).

Frederick WOODHOUSE: Colin Laverty, *Frederick Woodhouse and Sons: Australian Colonial Sporting Painters* (Sydney: David Ell Press, 1980).